GREAT WOMEN OF ACHIEVEMENT

Women in Space Who Changed the World

SONIA GUELDENPFENNIG

rosen publishing's
rosen
central
NEW YORK

This edition first published in 2012 by:

The Rosen Publishing Group, Inc.
29 East 21st Street
New York, NY 10010

Library of Congress Cataloging-in-Publication Data

Gueldenpfennig, Sonia.
Women in space who changed the world/Sonia Gueldenpfennig.
—1st ed.
p. cm.—(Great women of achievement)
Includes bibliographical references and index.
ISBN 978-1-4488-5998-6 (library binding)
1. Women astronauts—Biography—Juvenile literature. 2. Women in
astronautics—Biography—Juvenile literature. I. Title.
TL793.G84 2012
629.450092'52—dc23

2011033903

Manufactured in the United States of America

CPSIA Compliance Information: Batch #W12YA: For further information, contact Rosen Publishing, New
York, New York, at 1-800-237-9932.

First published by Second Story Press, Canada, 2005. Copyright © Sonia Gueldenpfennig, 2004.

Niki Walker, Editor

Contents

Introduction 5

Chapter 1 CAROLINE HERSCHEL 11

Chapter 2 JERRIE COBB 19

Chapter 3 VALENTINA TERESHKOVA 30

Chapter 4 SALLY RIDE 39

Chapter 5 ROBERTA BONDAR 49

Chapter 6 ELLEN OCHOA 58

Chapter 7 EILEEN COLLINS 67

Chapter 8 JULIE PAYETTE 74

Chapter 9 CHIAKI MUKAI 83

Chapter 10 KALPANA CHAWLA 91

Chapter 11 NADEZHDA KUZHELNAYA 101

Glossary 108
For More Information 110
For Further Reading 114
Index 116

Introduction

"**F**ive ... four ... three ... We have booster ignition and liftoff of *Columbia*, reaching new heights for women!" announced mission control as the shuttle blasted off into the summer night. It was June 23, 1999, and Commander Eileen Collins, the astronaut in charge of *Columbia*'s mission, had just made history. She was the first woman to lead a crew into space.

"We have come a long way," Sally Ride, the first American woman to travel in space, said about Eileen's mission. The Mercury Thirteen, a group of women who had fought unsuccessfully to go to space a generation earlier, were also there to cheer Eileen on. Commanding a crew had been the last job left for female astronauts to accomplish. Women have piloted shuttles, performed scientific experiments in space, and helped build a space station. They've captured and released satellites, designed space equipment, and performed space walks.

It hasn't been easy for women to secure their place in space exploration. They had to overcome the belief that science, technology, and exploration were men's domains and that women belonged in less dangerous and less difficult fields.

Space exploration began centuries before people launched the first spaceships into orbit. For thousands of years, astronomers searched the sky, looking for new discoveries and trying to make sense of the universe. History books are filled with the names of male scientists, but that doesn't mean women weren't involved. Women have always played a part in learning about space.

Commander Eileen Collins guides the space shuttle Columbia and leads its five-person crew on a successful mission to launch an X-ray telescope.

It wasn't easy for women to be included in the field of astronomy, especially hundreds of years ago, when few women were educated in math and science. Astronomy is the study of objects beyond Earth. Although a few women, such as Margaret Cavendish (1623–1673), became well-known astronomers, women usually worked without any recognition. Some worked with male relatives, assisting them in making observations and performing calculations. Often, women's discoveries were credited to the men with whom they worked. Many people thought that women were incapable of the reasoning and thinking that science required, so they couldn't believe that women could make scientific discoveries on their own. Even when women did claim recognition for their work, people often didn't believe that it was theirs. When Maria Cunitz wrote a book of astronomical tables in 1650, her husband wrote the preface for it, telling readers that it was not his work but hers.

It took centuries, but women gradually earned more opportunities to learn and to prove themselves as scientists. By the end of the 1800s, schools had opened for girls and women, and attitudes about what women could do, and should be free to do, were slowly changing. In the United States, Vassar College opened in 1861. Marie Mitchell was the director of its observatory from 1865 to 1888. She also became the first female member of the American Association for the Advancement of Science and the American Academy of Arts and Sciences.

In the late 1800s, Wilhelmina Fleming found work at the Harvard College Observatory. She was a new immigrant and single mother with few options open to her. A Harvard astronomer hired her to be his maid, but he soon recognized her aptitude for meticulous calculations and trained her to be his assistant. By the end of her career, she had devised a system for classifying stars and was curator of Harvard's astronomical photograph collection!

Despite the success of women like Wilhelmina and Marie, most people still thought of math and science as men's work, and believed that women belonged at home raising their families. Some women were prevented outright from being scientists and others were made to feel badly about their work. It took great strength to go against popular ideas of what women should do with their lives.

The twentieth century brought a new world of opportunities and challenges for women. More women than ever began earning university degrees and making contributions to science, but their numbers were still small. Many women found it difficult to find positions in universities and research centers. A common complaint was that a woman

Bessie Coleman was the first African-American pilot. She was born in 1892 to a family of sharecroppers in Atlanta, Texas. Because no American flight school would accept her as a Black woman, she moved to France in 1919 for her training. She performed exhibition flights and gave lectures across the United States, refusing to appear unless the audience was desegregated (meaning no separate areas or facilities for Black people and white people). She was killed during a test flight in 1926, but inspired many others to take up flying.

had to work twice as hard as her male colleagues to get half the credit.

Female pilots found that the same was true in the new field of aviation, or flight. Although women helped develop planes, and a few, such as Amelia Earhart, became well-known pilots, people felt that flying planes was a man's job and that women shouldn't do anything so complicated and dangerous. This belief existed into the 1950s, when people made the jump from flying airplanes to flying spacecraft.

The space age began in 1957, when the Soviet Union put the first satellite, called *Sputnik*, into orbit. Suddenly, space didn't seem so far away. It was no longer a place you could explore only through a telescope. People began imagining what it would be like to fly in space, go to the moon, and even visit other planets. Four years later, the dream of exploring space began to come true, when Yuri Gagarin became the first person to orbit Earth. Neil Armstrong accomplished the next major goal for human space flight when he became the first person on the moon in 1969. Millions of people all over the world learned about these amazing accomplishments and dreamed of following their heroes into space. The urge to push the limits and explore more of space—the "final frontier"—had become a powerful one. It's still powerful today, more than fifty years later.

Space flight has come a long way since the 1960s, but astronauts still face physical danger every time they head into orbit. Over the years, many astronauts and cosmonauts have died in accidents. Being an astronaut demands years of training and long hours of work. To pursue their training, many must uproot their lives and their families, leaving behind their homes, friends, and careers in other fields. It's

These six women were selected in 1978 as NASA's first female astronaut candidates. They are (left to right) Shannon Lucid, Margaret Seddon, Kathryn Sullivan, Judith Resnik, Anna Fisher, and Sally Ride. All went on to fly on shuttle missions.

a lot to give up. Most astronauts and cosmonauts would tell you that the risks and hard work are worth it, though. They get the chance to do important scientific work, help expand our understanding, explore the universe, and see the Earth from space. It makes all of the sacrifices seem like a small price to pay!

There have always been women who were willing to make the sacrifices and undergo the testing and training to become astronauts, but they were basically excluded from space flight for decades. Only one woman, Valentina Tereshkova, made it into space during the first twenty years of human space flight. Today, it is so common to see a woman on a space mission that it's easy to forget that women haven't always had a place in space programs. And although women have made great strides in space science and exploration in the last thirty years, they still represent a minority of astronauts and space scientists.

This book tells the story of eleven pioneering women from around the world whose skill and determination made a place for themselves, and others, in space. Some of these women fought hard for the chance to reach space; others confidently changed assumptions about the role of women in science and technology. All of these women have worked hard to realize their dreams, and they all share a strong dedication and passion for their work. Each of them serves as an example of what we can accomplish with hard work, determination, and a belief in ourselves. No one knows how far humans may travel in the future. If the next generation of space explorers follows the example of these women, the distance is sure to be limitless.

Chapter 1

Caroline Herschel

1750–1848

Space exploration began centuries ago, long before the first spaceships were invented. The earliest astronomers explored the night sky with their eyes and tried to explain what they saw of the universe. In the 1600s and 1700s, astronomers were able to see farther into space than ever before, as better and stronger telescopes were invented. Astronomers at this time discovered many stars, comets, and planets that had never been seen before. Caroline Herschel was one of these astronomers. She lived and worked at a time when few women were educated in science and even fewer were recognized for their scientific work.

Caroline Lucretia Herschel was born in the city of Hanover, in what is now Germany, on March 16, 1750. She was the second youngest of six children. Caroline was lucky to survive her childhood. She suffered from life-threatening diseases twice. When she was three years old, she caught smallpox, a disease that causes blisters to form on the body and is often fatal. It left her face deeply scarred and her left eye disfigured. At the age of ten, Caroline contracted typhus. She recovered, but the illness caused her to stop growing. Caroline remained four feet, three inches tall for the rest of her life.

Caroline's father, Isaac, was a professional musician. He played the oboe and became the bandmaster of the Hanovarian Foot Guards. Isaac did not have much formal education, but he was deeply interested in music, philosophy, and astronomy, and he enjoyed discussing these subjects with his children. When Caroline was a young girl, she loved to fall asleep listening to her father and her older brothers discuss the work of famous scientists like Isaac Newton.

Although Caroline's father valued education, her mother did not. She grudgingly agreed to allow her sons to be educated, but she did not feel that it was necessary for Caroline. Like most people of that time, Mrs. Herschel believed that teaching girls anything besides practical homemaking skills was a waste of time. Girls were expected to marry and become mothers and homemakers. Although Caroline's parents didn't think that she would ever marry because of her scars and small body, Mrs. Herschel still planned for her daughter to keep house—hers.

While her brothers went to school, Caroline spent her days cooking and cleaning. Despite his wife's disapproval, Caroline's father managed to pass on his love of learning and passion for astronomy to Caroline. Caroline later wrote about how her father would take her outside "to make [her] acquainted with several of the beautiful constellations, after [they] had been gazing at a comet which had been visible."

Caroline's father left home to fight in a war in 1757. When he returned in 1760, he was in poor health and had little strength to encourage Caroline's interest in learning. Caroline was too busy performing household chores for her mother to devote much time to her education anyway.

After her father's death in 1767, sixteen-year-old Caroline

Telescopes work by collecting light from distant objects, focusing it into an image, and magnifying it for the viewer. There are various types of telescopes. To study astronomy, Caroline used a Newtonian telescope, a fairly simple version that uses mirrors to create the image. Although telescopes today are much more powerful than Caroline's, her telescope would have been impressive in her day.

realized that she was in danger of spending the rest of her life as her mother's maid. To try to escape this fate, she took lessons in dressmaking and trained to become a governess. Her responsibilities at home left her little time to train, however, and Caroline had to abandon those ambitions.

One of Caroline's brothers, William, had moved to England several years earlier to pursue a career in music. On a visit home, he saw how unhappy Caroline was, so he asked her to move with him to his home in Bath, England. Caroline adored her brother and eagerly accepted the offer, despite her mother's protests. She was excited to leave her mother's house to look after her brother's house instead. Unlike their mother, William would not treat Caroline like a servant.

William was a professional musician, just as their father had been. He taught Caroline how to sing, and before long she was performing with him and becoming a well-known soprano. She performed as many as five nights a week and could have made music a lifelong career. Besides singing,

William also began teaching Caroline English, mathematics, and astronomy.

Although William earned his living as a musician, he was more interested in studying the stars, and he devoted every spare moment to searching the night sky. One of the major aims of astronomers in the eighteenth century was to discover and catalog new objects in space. William soon became frustrated with the telescopes available at the time, so he began to make his own. Caroline became his assistant. She made molds for the telescope mirrors out of manure and then ground and polished the glass—a task that demanded perfect accuracy in order for the telescopes to work.

Caroline's lack of education made her shy about attempting any studies of the night sky on her own, but the more she learned about mathematics and the more she saw through William's telescopes, the more interested she became in observing the universe. Over time, she mastered geometry and algebra and learned how to do the calculations that astronomers used to figure out the location of stars and planets and how far away they are from Earth.

In Caroline's honor, a minor planet (asteroid) was named Lucretia in 1889, and in 1939 one of the moon's craters, pictured at right, was named C. Herschel.

Caroline Herschel is credited with discovering eight comets, three galaxies, and several open clusters (loose groupings of stars).

In 1781, William made his greatest discovery, one that would help change both his life and Caroline's. He found the planet Uranus, the first planet ever discovered with a telescope. The discovery was a major accomplishment, and it made him famous internationally. In 1782, King George III of England appointed William to be the royal astronomer and provided him with a salary that allowed him to give up his musical career and focus on astronomy full-time. William decided to move to Windsor to be closer to the king's court. Caroline did not want to sing without William, so she stopped performing, too. She decided to move to Windsor with William to continue being his assistant.

During this time, William gave Caroline a telescope of her own. Looking through the glass, she could get lost among the stars. She was especially interested in comets. Whenever she had a spare moment, she searched the night sky for anything new and unusual. She had little time for her own observations, though, since she had become an essential part of William's work. Caroline planned the schedule for each night's work, including the parts of the sky to observe. William usually used a telescope that was twenty feet long. On clear nights, he and Caroline gathered at the base of it, with William standing on a chair to see into it. He called out observations about stars, galaxies, asteroids, and other bodies, and Caroline carefully recorded everything. Later, she performed all of the calculations needed to determine each body's exact location in space. Although she had a natural ability for mathematics, Caroline never memorized the multiplication table. Instead, she did the complicated calculations using a card with the table written on it. Still, Caroline's calculations were incredibly accurate.

Caroline worked on her own observations only when William was away. On those nights, Caroline would go outside

Caroline observed her second comet in 1788. It was not seen again until 1939, when an astronomer named Roger Rigollet observed it. The comet, now called Herschel-Rigollet, takes 155 years to orbit the sun.

and make careful sweeps of the night sky with her telescope, looking for anything unusual. On February 26, 1783, she saw something that had never been seen before. It was a star cluster located near the constellation of Canis Major. It was the first of many discoveries Caroline would make over the years.

On August 1, 1786, Caroline made her most important discovery. She saw a point of light she had not noticed before in the constellation of Leo. The next night, she saw it again, and observed that its position had changed slightly in relation to the rest of the constellation. She was sure the point of light was a comet. Caroline sent letters to other astronomers, telling them of her amazing find, and they began tracking the comet as well. It soon became known as the "first lady's comet," and her discovery brought Caroline a bit of fame. A year later, King George III officially recognized her as William's assistant and provided her with a salary. She earned fifty pounds a year—one-fourth of what her brother earned. Still, the salary made Caroline the first woman to be appointed to a scientific position and to be paid for scientific work. More than anything, Caroline was thrilled to have made her own contribution to astronomy.

Caroline's happiness was soon tested, though. For years, she had taken care of her brother and his household. Her role and her life changed when William married a woman named Mary Pitt in 1788. Caroline moved out of her brother's house into nearby lodgings. She still went to William's house to work every day, but she resented losing her position in the household to Mary. Although Caroline had some difficulty getting used to the change, she eventually became friends with her new sister-in-law. When

William and Mary had a son named John in 1792, she eagerly devoted herself to helping raise him. During the next decade, Caroline was kept busy helping with John's education and her brother's work, but she still found time for her own studies and discovered seven more comets.

John Herschel, Caroline's nephew, was a mathematician, lawyer, teacher, chemist, and civil servant, as well as an astronomer. He is most famous for his work on double stars, two stars that are so close together that they appear to be one.

Caroline's work was interesting, but she wanted a new challenge. She turned her attention to the work of an astronomer named Flamsteed, who had lived a century earlier. Flamsteed had made a catalog of stars, called *Historia coelestis Britannica*. Other astronomers used this book to help them identify what they saw. Caroline knew that the book was missing many known stars and needed to be updated. She cross-referenced the stars in the catalog and made corrections where new information had been found. In total, she cataloged 560 additional stars. In 1798, she finished the updated edition, titled *Index to Flamsteed's Observations of the Fixed Stars*, and presented it to the Royal Astronomical Society. At forty-seven years of age, she thought that the book would be her life's major achievement. Satisfied, she decided to put aside her independent work and turn her attention back to William and John. John eventually grew up to become a famous astronomer, partly because of the attention that his aunt focused on his education.

Caroline continued to assist William until his death in 1822. She then returned to her hometown of Hanover, where she spent the rest of her life. There, she completed a project that William had begun before his death, a catalog of nebulae. Nebulae are clouds of dust and gas where stars form. By the time Caroline finished the catalog, it contained more than 2,500 nebulae. The work was published in 1827

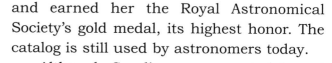

Caroline's gravestone says, "The eyes of her who is glorified below turned to the starry heaven." Caroline wrote these words so that people would remember how much she loved space.

and earned her the Royal Astronomical Society's gold medal, its highest honor. The catalog is still used by astronomers today.

Although Caroline never wanted to put her own work ahead of William's or John's, she became an accomplished independent researcher whose work earned many honors. She and another female scientist, Mary Somerville, were made the first honorary female members of the Royal Society in 1835 (women were not allowed to become full members until 1945). She was made an honorary member of the Royal Irish Academy in 1838, and in 1846, on her ninety-sixth birthday, she received the Gold Medal for Science from the King of Prussia in honor of her life's work.

Even as an old woman, Caroline still had lots of energy. During one of his visits, John wrote, "She runs about the town with me, and skips up her two flights of stairs." She also enjoyed talking with other astronomers. She had become a well-known and respected astronomer, and many scientists visited her to share their love of space.

Caroline's career was unusual at a time when few women were educated in the areas of mathematics and science, and even fewer became scientists. By the time she died on January 9, 1848, at the age of 97, Caroline had challenged many assumptions about what women were capable of doing.

Chapter 2

Jerrie Cobb

1931–

W hen the first airplanes took to the air at the start of the 1900s, they were rickety inventions that couldn't fly very far or very high. Looking at them today, it's hard to believe that they could leave the ground, let alone stay in the air. Airplanes were improved upon quickly, though, and they constantly stretched the limits of flight. It wasn't long before airplanes were stretching the limits of people's imaginations as well.

Geraldyn "Jerrie" Cobb was one of those people. She was born in Norman, Oklahoma, in 1931, when the airplane was still a fairly new invention. Jerrie was nine years old when her father, an Air Force officer and pilot, took her on her first ride in a plane. "Even before the old [plane] had reached 300 feet (91.4 meters)," she recalled, "I recognized the sky would be my home." She longed to be in control of a plane and begged her father to give her flying lessons. When she was twelve years old, he agreed.

Jerrie was a shy and quiet child. She had been born with an extra membrane in her mouth that made it difficult for her to speak clearly. When she started kindergarten, her parents decided to have it removed. Jerrie was stubborn, though, and it took three trips to the doctor before she let them operate. Afterward, Jerrie still felt awkward talking, and she avoided speaking whenever possible.

School was a nightmare for Jerrie. Answering questions in class and talking with other children were hard for her. When she was fourteen, she began to skip school. When her parents found out, her father made her a deal: If she would go to school, she could continue taking flying lessons. Jerrie agreed. She would do anything to fly. On her sixteenth birthday—the first day she was eligible—she got her pilot's license.

After finishing high school, Jerrie convinced her parents to let her work instead of going to college. She wanted to make her living as a professional pilot, but she knew that she needed more practice before she would be skilled enough. In the meantime, she earned money in other ways. The Oklahoma City Queens, a semiprofessional team in the women's National Softball League, hired her to play second base. Unlike playing in professional sports today, it wasn't a glamorous job, but Jerrie was content—the job paid enough for her to continue flying.

Still, her parents had not given up trying to convince Jerrie to go to college. She reluctantly agreed to go to the Oklahoma College for Women. Jerrie quickly decided that she didn't like college any better than she had liked high school. Her shyness still made it hard for her to fit in and to participate in class. She even walked out of a public-speaking class rather than have to make a speech in front of her classmates. Jerrie didn't go back to the college after the first year.

Jerrie was determined to be a pilot, but in the 1950s it was hard for any pilot, much less a young woman with little experience, to find a job flying. During World War II, many soldiers had been taught to fly and when the war had ended, they found themselves competing for work. Jerrie didn't give up, though, and managed to make a living dusting crops, patrolling oil fields, and teaching.

Eventually, Jerrie found a job flying that was so dangerous and difficult that no one else wanted it. She delivered planes to South America, flying with little fuel over oceans, jungles, and mountains. On her first trip, she was arrested when she touched down in Ecuador in a Peruvian Air Force plane. Ecuador and Peru were at war at the time, and the Ecuadorian army mistakenly thought that she was a spy. Jerrie was kept in a jail cell for twelve days, not knowing what would happen to her. She was scared, but not scared enough to give up flying.

For the next two years, Jerrie ferried planes all over the world. She was doing what she loved—flying planes and having adventures. Jerrie quit the job in 1955, however, after breaking up with her boyfriend and boss, Jack Ford. She went home to Oklahoma.

During flying competitions, women pilots were expected to dress like "ladies" in high heels, dresses, and stockings. Jerrie found it impossible to fly dressed this way, so she sometimes changed clothes while she was flying, getting into and out of her flying gear before she landed.

Back in the United States, Jerrie began competing in air races and flying competitions. Between 1957 and 1960, she set three World Aviation Records. One was for speed, one was for distance, and on two occasions she set a record for absolute altitude. Jerrie loved to challenge what she and her planes could do.

While Jerrie was setting flying records, the United States was developing its space program. The country was desperate to send people into space. Its fiercest rival, the Soviet Union (Russia today), had already put the first satellite into orbit and was planning to send people into space. The Americans were anxious not to be left behind. In the late 1950s, the National Aeronautics and Space Administration (NASA) began looking for astronauts of its own. After a lot of searching and many physical tests, seven men were chosen to be the first astronauts. This group was called the Mercury Seven. Instantly, the men became national heroes.

One of the doctors who performed the tests on potential astronauts was Dr. Randy Lovelace. He was worried that, despite selecting astronauts, NASA would still be unable to send people into space. NASA was having trouble sending small satellites into orbit, and it would be even harder to launch a full-grown man in a large spacecraft. Lovelace began thinking about putting a smaller, lighter person into the spacecraft. Since women are generally smaller and lighter than men, he thought it made sense for women to be astronauts.

Lovelace heard about Jerrie and her impressive collection of flying records

NASA's Beginnings

The National Aeronautics and Space Administration (NASA) was established in 1958. Its first space program was called Project Mercury. The goal was to put human beings safely into space. NASA chose its first astronauts in 1959, and the first manned American space flight took place on May 5, 1961, when Alan Shepard flew above Earth's atmosphere in *Freedom 7*.

and thought that she would be an ideal astronaut candi-date. When he asked her to take the same tests that the Mercury Seven had taken, Jerrie was thrilled. This was a chance to help her country while proving her skills as a pilot at the same time.

The first round of tests was physical. Because no one had ever been into space before, scientists had to imagine what would happen to the human body at high speeds, at high altitudes, and in weightless conditions. They tested potential astronauts for every situation that they could think of. Jerrie underwent every test. She had very cold water injected into her inner ear to cause extreme dizziness. She was strapped with electrodes and rode a stationary bicycle until she was ready to collapse. She was crammed into a machine that measured her body's level of radiation, potas-sium, and muscle mass. At the same time, the machine weeded out candidates who suffered from claustrophobia. The Mercury spacecraft were just big enough for a seat and the controls. There was no room to stand up, stretch, or even leave the seat. Candidates had to prove that they could stand to be closed in a very small, cramped space.

The most grueling test of all, though, was the Multi-Axis Spin Test Inertia Facility (MASTIF). It was a simulator made up of three huge metal rings that moved independently of one another in different directions. Its movements simulat-ed a spacecraft spinning out of control. Jerrie was strapped to a seat at the center of it, facing a control panel. Once the simulator started, she was whipped around in all directions at a rate of thirty spins per minute. Being in the machine was like doing somersaults, cartwheels, and twirls all at the same time. By the time the simulator reached its full speed, Jerrie could barely see and her stomach was churning. She had to operate the controls and bring her "craft" out of each of the spins to make the sickening ride stop.

Jerrie tests the Multi-Axis Spin Test Inertia Facility, or MASTIF. The facility is installed in the Altitude Wind Tunnel at the Lewis Research Center, now the John H. Glenn Research Center.

In all of the tests, Jerrie did just as well, if not better, than the male astronauts. Lovelace was encouraged by her results, but he wanted to repeat his experiment on other women to make sure that Jerrie's success wasn't a one-in-a-million performance. With Jerrie's help, he found other female pilots who were as eager as Jerrie for the chance to become astronauts.

Word got out that a group of women might become astronauts, and soon people wanted to know all about them. Jerrie, who was still very shy, was uncomfortable talking to reporters, but she knew that it was part of an astronaut's job. After all, everything that the Mercury Seven did was photographed and written about. Questions about the tests and her dreams of flying in space were easy to answer, but Jerrie was surprised that anyone wanted to know about her personal life. One reporter even asked her if she could cook. What did that have to do with being an astronaut?

People were intrigued by the "girl astronauts," as they were often called. In 1960, it was expected that a woman would get married, have children, and run her household. Women pilots were rare, and those who could make a living flying had to work very hard to keep their jobs. Despite the interest in the female astronaut candidates, most people did not take them very seriously. They didn't think that women could have the technical knowledge or mechanical skill needed to fly a plane, never mind a spacecraft.

Determined to prove that she had what it took to fly in space, Jerrie took two more sets of astronaut tests. The first set was psychological tests. The doctors wanted to know if her mind could handle the loneliness and pressures of space flight. An important part of these tests was the isolation experiment. Jerrie was put in a tank of warm water in a pitch-black room that blocked out all outside contact— sounds, smells, and even vibrations. It can be very unnerving being cut off from the rest of the world. The goal of the experiment was to stay in the pool for as long as possible. Jerrie's time of nine hours and forty minutes was a new record and more than three hours longer than any of the Mercury Seven had lasted. Her shy, quiet nature had prepared her well for this experiment.

The next set of tests took place at the naval base in Pensacola, Florida. There, Jerrie used the equipment that military test pilots and the Mercury Seven trained on. She felt what it was like to fly at high altitudes, to eject from an aircraft, and to escape from a "crashed" space capsule that was underwater. Once again, Jerrie proved that she could perform these tasks as well as any man.

Meanwhile, Dr. Lovelace made plans to continue the testing with the rest of the women, who had nicknamed themselves the Mercury Thirteen. Just before the rest of the Mercury Thirteen were supposed to go to Pensacola, though, the plans were suddenly canceled. At first, Jerrie and the other women could not get a reason for the cancellation. Jerrie was determined to find out what had happened, so she traveled to the naval base and then to Washington, D.C., for answers. Finally, she learned that the tests had been canceled because NASA did not want to run them on women. At first, NASA wouldn't say why, but eventually the agency stated that the seven men it had already trained were enough and it didn't have any plans for female astronauts. Jerrie and the other women had to face the possibility that they might never fly in space.

Jerrie refused to give up her dream, though. She knew that the Mercury Thirteen would be great astronauts. They were all physically fit and strong, had experience flying all sorts of aircraft, and had personalities that thrived in high-pressure situations. The only thing that was standing in their way was the idea that women didn't belong in space. With the help of Janey Hart, one of the Mercury Thirteen and the wife of a senator, Jerrie arranged a special hearing of the Space Committee in July of 1962. The aim of the hearing was to officially determine the qualifications for selecting astronauts.

Despite her fear of public speaking, Jerrie testified before the committee, explaining how well she and the other women did on the tests and how experienced they were as

Marion Wallace "Wally" Funk volunteered to take the astronaut tests after learning about Jerrie's amazing results. When the program was canceled, Wally was so determined to complete the tests that she arranged to take them privately. When she was not provided with a pressure suit to ride in the centrifuge, she improvised by borrowing her mother's girdle. She hoped that the close-fitting garment would keep her from passing out. The girdle probably did more harm than good, but Wally passed the test anyway.

pilots. Jerrie spoke very elo-
quently, saying, "We seek only
a place in our nation's space
future without discrimination.
We ask as citizens of this
nation to be allowed to participate with seriousness and
sincerity in the making of history now." She argued that, at
the very least, the Mercury
Thirteen should be allowed to
continue the tests so that they
would be ready if NASA decided it needed more astronauts.

The committee later
heard from NASA's representatives. George Low, a NASA director, insisted that it was necessary to accept only people who
had been jet test pilots. Jet test
pilots were trained to take risks

*Jerrie poses beside a
Mercury spaceship capsule,
which as a woman she was
never able to ride into
space despite passing all
the required tests.*

and make quick decisions while flying unfamiliar aircraft.
NASA did not believe that this kind of experience could be
achieved any other way. Astronauts John Glenn and Scott
Carpenter also testified and agreed with Low. Although
NASA and its representatives claimed that the decision to
refuse female candidates was not based on gender, John
Glenn stated, "It is just a fact. The men go off and fight the
wars and fly the airplanes and come back and help design
and build and test them. The fact that women are not in this
field is a fact of our social order."

In the end, the committee sided with NASA. Astronaut
candidates would have to be jet test pilots. Since the only
way to become a jet test pilot was through the military and
the military didn't let women fly jets, it was impossible for a

woman to have the qualifications that NASA wanted. Jerrie would not be going into space. Still, she refused to give up. She lectured about her cause, got magazines and newspapers to write about her, and sent letters to NASA asking to be allowed in the astronaut program.

The Mercury Thirteen

The members of the Mercury Thirteen were Jerrie Cobb, Myrtle "K" Cagle, Jan Dietrich, Marion Dietrich, Wally Funk, Janey Hart, Jean Nixon, Gene Nora Jessen, Irene Leverton, Sarah Gorelick Rutley, Bernice "B" Steadman, Jerri Sloan Truhill, and Rhea Allison Woltman. For the chance to become astronauts, many of these women lost their hard-won flying jobs and left behind their families for a time.

Seven of the Mercury Thirteen visited the Kennedy Space Center in 1995, and are shown in the photograph above: (left to right) Gene Nora Jessen, Wally Funk, Jerrie Cobb, Jerri Truhill, Sarah Rutley, Myrtle Cagle, and Bernice Steadman.

In 1965, after years of unsuccessfully trying to convince NASA, Jerrie took a job flying in South America again. She joined a group of Christian missionaries in the Amazon rain forest, delivering food, medicine, and other items to areas that could only be reached by plane. Although she still dreamed about flying in space, she dedicated herself to helping others in the meantime. Her humanitarian work earned Jerrie a Nobel Peace Prize nomination in 1981.

In 1998, the first American in space, John Glenn, returned to space as part of a mission to compare the effects of space and old age on the human body. After hearing that a seventy-seven-year-old could go into space, Jerrie hoped that she might get a second chance. "I would give my life to fly in space," Jerrie said. "I would have then. I would now." People from around the world heard of Jerrie's cause and tried to convince NASA to send her into space. Unfortunately, she was once again denied the opportunity. Nevertheless, the world continues to acknowledge Jerrie's achievements. In 2000, she was inducted into the Women in Aviation's Pioneer Hall of Fame. And in 2007, the University of Wisconsin gave her an honorary doctorate of sciences.

Although Jerrie will probably never fly in space, she has been an inspiration to countless women, and her effort made it easier for other women to become astronauts. When Eileen Collins became the first female astronaut to command a mission in 1999, she acknowledged the contribution of the Mercury Thirteen by inviting the women to watch her launch. Although Jerrie was not aboard the shuttle that day, she knew that her struggle was acknowledged and appreciated by the women who were living her dream.

Chapter 3
Valentina Tereshkova

1937–

When the possibility of space exploration became real in the middle of the twentieth century, the United States and the Soviet Union began competing to be the first country to reach space. The countries were in the midst of the Cold War, and each one wanted to show the rest of the world that it was the superior country. Being the first country in space, and to reach the moon, would prove that the country had the best technology and the greatest scientific knowledge. This competition became known as the space race.

When the Soviet Union launched Yuri Gagarin into space in 1961, it seemed that the Soviets would win the race. The United States, however, was determined not to be left too far behind. It soon caught up to the Soviet Union by launching John Glenn into orbit in 1962. The Soviet Union had to find new ways to impress the world. It decided to send the first woman into space. Valentina Tereshkova would be that woman.

Valentina was born on March 6, 1937, in the town of Maslennikovo in the northwest part of the Soviet Union. Her father had been a tractor driver and then a soldier. He was killed during World War II when Valentina was only two years old. Her mother, Elena, raised Valentina, her older sister, Ludmilla, and her younger brother, Vladimir, by herself. "She put all her strength and health" into raising the children, Valentina has said.

Valentina's childhood was a difficult time as the family struggled to survive on a meager income. They received only "a 50-ruble benefit per each child, while a loaf of bread cost 200 rubles," Valentina remembers. To help, she began working at an early age. Valentina did not start school until she was ten years old, but she quickly caught up with the other students her age. After high school, Valentina spent a short time working at a tire factory before going to work with her mother and her sister

The Cold War was a period of strong tensions between the West, especially the United States, and the Soviet Union. It lasted from the end of World War II to the early 1990s. At the heart of the conflict were very different ideas about how countries should be run. The West supported capitalism, while the Soviets believed in communism. Both sides were convinced that the other was set on controlling the world. Each side built up huge stores of weapons, including nuclear weapons, and competed to prove that it was more powerful and more advanced than the other. The Cold War ended with the collapse of the Soviet Union.

in a textile mill. With her first paycheck from this job, she bought her mother a shawl as a gift. Valentina wanted to continue her education, so she took classes through correspondence while working. She eventually earned a certificate in cotton-spinning technology.

Valentina was hard-working, but she also enjoyed spending time with friends and co-workers in her free time. Craving thrills and adventure, she joined the Yaroslavl Air Sports Club, a local group that organized parachute jumps. Valentina made her first parachute jump in 1959 when she was eighteen years old and quickly fell in love with the sport. She was soon doing more daring and more difficult jumps and began performing with the group at local fairs. Eager to share her new hobby with more people, Valentina started a parachute club for workers at the textile mill. By 1961, she had made one hundred jumps.

That same year, Valentina became inspired by Yuri Gagarin's historic flight and began to dream of exploring space herself. She wrote to the Central Committee of the Communist Party and volunteered to become a cosmonaut. The committee had been planning to send a woman into space and was searching for women with the types of experience that cosmonauts needed. Although the committee received thousands of letters just like hers, Valentina's letter stood out. She wasn't a pilot like Gagarin, but Valentina's amazing parachuting record caught the committee's attention. Since Soviet space capsules crashed to the ground when they returned from orbit, cosmonauts had to know how to parachute out of them before impact. Valentina's experience was ideal, and the committee selected her to become one of five female cosmonaut candidates.

Valentina eagerly reported for cosmonaut training along with four other women. The government did not want the United States to know what it was planning, so the project was kept top secret. Valentina was not allowed to tell even her mother about it. When she left to begin her training, Valentina told her mother that she had been selected to join a special skydiving team. This was not a complete lie—it was her parachuting experience that had gotten her selected.

Yuri Gagarin, the famous cosmonaut, would be helping to train the female candidates and was part of the group that would choose which cosmonaut would go into space. Valentina was thrilled to be working so closely with her hero. She did well at the physical training, especially the many parachute jumps that were required. She also took flights that mimicked the feeling of weightlessness, spent days in isolation experiments, and learned to fly a jet.

One of the more unpleasant parts of the training involved riding in a centrifuge. This machine consisted of a small cabin that spun in a circle at high speeds, creating a lot of force against the rider's body. Earlier cosmonauts had nicknamed it "the devil's merry-go-round." The device prepared cosmonauts for what they would feel when they launched into space. Although riding in the centrifuge was incredibly unpleasant and uncomfortable, Valentina didn't let her discomfort show. She didn't want anyone to think that a girl couldn't handle the ride. She kept smiling until the force of the centrifuge distorted her face so much that no one could tell what expression she had on it. When she got out of the cabin, she was cheerful and joked with the technicians.

Besides the hours of physical training, Valentina's training also required classroom time. Valentina and the other candidates learned how rockets and spacecraft get into and stay in orbit. This area of study is known as rocket theory. They also studied the engineering, or design and

The term "cosmonaut" comes from the Greek word "cosmos," meaning "universe," and "naut," meaning "sailor."

construction, of spacecraft. "It was hard for her to master rocket techniques, study spaceship designs and equipment, but she tackled the job stubbornly and devoted much of her own time to study, poring over books and notes in the evening," Gagarin later said with admiration.

Valentina faced stiff competition among the other women in the group, who were all pilots. Most of them had college degrees. Although Valentina was impressed by her fellow candidates, she never became discouraged. She was determined to master her cosmonaut training. She worked hard, asking for help when she needed it and showing her enthusiasm for the project. Her efforts paid off. Although some people felt that Valentina Ponomaryova was the most qualified woman in the group, Valentina Tereshkova was chosen to become the world's first female in space.

Valentina's mission would be the Soviet's second joint flight, which is when two space capsules orbit Earth at the

Three women cosmonauts, (left to right) Valentina Ponomaryova, Irina Solovyeva, and Valentina Tereshkova, stand together before the launching of Vostok 6 *on June 16, 1963.*

same time. One of the goals was to improve spacecraft operation during joint flights. Valeri Bykovsky launched in the first capsule, *Vostok 5*, on June 14, 1963. On June 16, 1963, Valentina Tereshkova blasted off aboard *Vostok 6*, and less than ten minutes later was in orbit. Using the call sign "Chaika," which is Russian for "seagull," Valentina radioed to Earth, "I see the horizon. A light blue, a beautiful band. This is the Earth. How beautiful it is. All goes well." Seeing the world from this perspective filled her with wonder. In her logbook, she wrote about a storm that she saw over the Indian Ocean: "Before each sunrise there is a unique sight. The clouds over the ocean have the form of ridges and more often, of streets with small breaks in them." Only from space could she imagine that the clouds are made up of city streets.

While the main goal of the mission was to send a woman into orbit to monitor her body's reaction to space travel, Valentina was expected to do more than just sit aboard her Vostok capsule. She had tasks to perform, such as making observations of Earth, the moon, and stars, performing biological experiments, and testing capsule equipment. Although Valentina performed many of her assigned tasks, she was criticized for leaving some unfinished. As a result, officials decided not to allow Valentina to take control of the capsule as they'd originally planned.

By the end of her mission, Valentina had orbited Earth 48 times. She spent 2 days, 22 hours, and 50 minutes in space—longer than all of the American space flights put together. Valentina got

The Vostok spacecraft were the first to take people into space. Only one person could fit inside the tube-shaped crafts, which were 17 feet (5 meters) long and 9 feet (2.7 meters) wide. They had enough life support to last ten days in orbit. In total, there were six flights aboard Vostok spacecraft. The first was Yuri Gagarin's and the last was Valentina Tereshkova's.

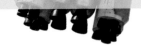

to fly longer than she had expected. "I was proud and happy that I stayed in space for three instead of the planned two days," she says.

When it was time to return to Earth, Valentina performed the demanding task of guiding her spacecraft into position for re-entering the atmosphere. When her spacecraft was 10,000 feet (3,048 meters) above the ground, Valentina ejected from the capsule. All of the jumps she had made in the past paid off and she parachuted expertly to the ground. Only for a moment did she worry that she would land in the lake beside the field that she was aiming for. When she touched down in farm fields in Kazakhstan, the local people rushed out to meet her. It wasn't every day that a woman dropped out of the sky!

Despite some problems, the flight of *Vostok 6* was a success. Valentina had been able to talk with Valeri Bykovsky in *Vostok 5* by radio, and the two capsules came within a few miles of each other. This joint flight provided valuable information to scientists and engineers who had plans for docking spacecraft in orbit. Docking is when two spacecraft join together. The biggest benefit of the mission, though, was proving that women were physically capable of space flight.

Valentina, like more than half of all astronauts and cosmonauts, suffered from space motion sickness for a part of her flight. Similar to regular motion sickness, it's caused by a person's vestibular, or balance, system trying to adapt to an environment in which there's no sense of what's up and what's down.

Life changed dramatically for Valentina after her mission. When she was taken from the landing site, she was questioned by officials and tested by doctors and scientists. Valentina received the Order of Lenin and Hero of the Soviet Union awards and was given an honorary commission in the Soviet Air Force. She then traveled around the globe, giving press conferences and interviews about her experience in space. People wanted to know everything about her. The whole world was fascinated by this textile worker who had become the first woman in space. Although the attention was overwhelming and her schedule became tiring, Valentina was proud of her flight and happy to share her experience with others.

In the middle of all this activity, Valentina married Andrian Nikolayev, a cosmonaut she had met during her training. Some people claim that she and Andrian were pressured to get married, to create more publicity for the Soviet space program. Many important people in the Soviet Union went to their wedding, including the premier, Nikita Khrushchev. In 1964, the couple had a baby girl named Elena Andrianovna. She was the first person in the world whose parents had both been in space. Valentina and Andrian separated soon after Elena was born.

Valentina wanted to continue her career in the space program. To advance her skills and knowledge, she enrolled in the Zhukovsky Military Air Academy and studied aviation engineering. Unfortunately, after she graduated in 1969, the government ended the female cosmonaut unit. Valentina never had another opportunity to go to space.

She became active in the Communist Party and eventually held high-ranking positions in the Soviet government. She also spoke about women's issues, such as the working conditions women faced. She served as the Chair of the Soviet Women Committee and, in 1975, she represented the Soviet Union at the United Nations World Conference of the International Women's Year. Valentina was awarded several honors for her work outside the space program. Among these are the United Nations Gold Medal of Peace, the Simba International Women's Movement Award, and the Joliot-Curie Gold Medal.

Although Valentina represented the Soviet Union's promise of equality between men and women, she is now

A crater on the moon is named after Valentina, and an asteroid bears the name "Seagull," in honor of her radio name during her space flight.

To this day, Valentina Tereshkova is the only woman to have made a solo space flight.

critical of the space program's treatment of women cosmonauts. She told a Russian newspaper, "They forbade me from flying despite my protests and arguments. After being once in space, I was desperately keen to go back there. But it didn't happen." In fact, no Soviet woman traveled to space for almost two decades. Many people now believe the female cosmonauts were meant to be a novelty, another "first" that the Soviet Union could claim over the United States. None of the female cosmonauts Valentina trained with were ever fully accepted into the Soviet space program.

Valentina officially retired as a cosmonaut in 1997, but she has remained active in public life. Valentina was invited to Russian President Vladmir Putin's home for her seventieth birthday. There she said she wouldn't mind one day going to Mars, even if it could only be a one-way trip. Valentina continues to be a symbol of Russia's achievements. She even carried a torch in the 2008 Summer Olympics Torch Relay in St. Petersburg, Russia. Of her work, Valentina says, "[E]veryone should do what he or she is good at. They should do what they love. I always did what I loved—in the space program and in my present work. I enjoy introducing foreign governments to [Russia's] achievements in the areas of culture, science, and technology." Although she enjoys her work today, she will never forget the days she spent orbiting Earth. As she has said, "Anyone who has spent any time in space will love it for the rest of their lives."

Chapter 4

Sally Ride

1951–

For decades, the American astronaut program was off limits to women. Although women like Jerrie Cobb tried to break down barriers in NASA's early days, it wasn't until the 1970s that female astronaut candidates were finally accepted. Sally Ride was among those first female astronauts. She became famous as the first American woman to reach space, and she has helped pave the way for many more female astronauts to follow.

Sally Kristen Ride was born in Los Angeles, California, on May 26, 1951. Her mother was a counselor in a women's prison and her father was a college professor. They taught Sally and her younger sister, Karen, to believe that they were capable of doing almost anything. At a time when many people believed that science and sports were boys' domains, Sally's parents encouraged her to explore her interests, which included chemistry sets and playing baseball and football with the boys in her neighborhood.

At a young age, Sally thought that she had figured out what she wanted to be when she grew up—a professional tennis player. She began playing when she was ten and spent many hours practicing. By the time she was in her teens, Sally was ranked eighteenth on the national junior tennis circuit.

Although she spent a lot of time practicing tennis, Sally also took school seriously and earned excellent grades. After graduating from high school in 1968, she enrolled at Swarthmore College to study physics. After her first year of college, Sally decided to take time off from school to pursue a career in tennis. Within three months, though, she realized that she would never be good enough to turn pro. Sally decided that she would do better following a career in science.

Sally didn't return to Swarthmore, but instead transferred to Stanford University, which is in her home state. As a break from the experiments, formulas, and calculations in her science classes, she took classes in English Literature. When Sally graduated in 1973, she earned two degrees: a Bachelor of Science in Physics and a Bachelor of Arts in English.

After earning her bachelor degrees, Sally stayed at Stanford University and worked toward earning graduate degrees. In 1977, she completed a doctorate (Ph.D.) in astrophysics, the study of the physics and chemistry of celestial bodies such as stars and comets. During her last weeks at the school, Sally read an ad in the university newspaper about a search for new astronauts. She had always been interested in space, but this was the first time she had considered going there. She decided to apply to NASA and was accepted.

Of the thousands of people who applied to the space program that year, NASA accepted twenty-nine men and six women. This group began a year-long program of training and evaluation in the summer of 1978. They skydived, learned how to survive in water, and rode in simulators that prepared them for liftoff and living in weightlessness. They also studied navigation and radio communication and learned all about NASA's new vehicles, the space shuttles. During this time, Sally also earned her pilot's license, and flying quickly became one of her favorite hobbies.

After finishing her first year of training, Sally began a second stage of training known as a technical assignment. "It takes a couple of years just to get the background and knowledge that you need before you can go into detailed training for [a] flight," she explains. Her first jobs as an astronaut were as part of the ground crew for the second and third missions of the space shuttle *Columbia*, in 1981 and 1982. She was the Capsule Communicator, or CAPCOM, for each of the missions. It was her job to radio messages between mission control—the people running the shuttle from the ground—and the shuttle crew. During her technical assignment, Sally also helped design a robotic arm for the shuttle, which would allow astronauts aboard the shuttle to grab and move objects in space.

Columbia was the first space shuttle to make a flight, in 1981. Shuttles are the first spacecraft designed to be reused. The complete fleet of space shuttles included *Columbia, Atlantic, Challenger, Discovery, Endeavor,* and *Enterprise.*

When Sally received news of her first flight assignment, she found that she had even more to learn. Astronauts not only have to know how to operate every aspect of the shuttle, but they also have to be prepared for every possible emergency. They must also train and practice for the specific tasks of their mission, such as releasing satellites. "The most difficult part of astronaut training is learning everything that you need to know so that you are an expert on every detail of the space shuttle and the experiments. So it's a lot like being in school in a very difficult course," she says. For her first mission, Sally's duties were to deploy two satellites, conduct trials of the robotic arm she had helped design, and perform and monitor about forty scientific experiments.

Sally spent more than a year preparing for her first mission, which lifted off on June 18, 1983, amid the cheers of an enormous crowd. Hours before the launch, Sally and her crewmates began the journey from the astronaut quarters at the Kennedy Space Center in Florida to the launch pad. After arriving at the site, Sally and the rest of the crew entered an elevator that carried them up the launch tower to a chamber connected to the shuttle. Technicians were waiting for them onboard. They were the only people around for miles.

The astronauts put on their harnesses and helmets and got strapped into their seats in the shuttle. With everyone secure, the technicians left. There was

Spacesuits

NASA astronauts wear orange partial-pressure suits during launch and re-entry to protect themselves in case the cabin loses pressure. For spacewalks, astronauts wear Extravehicular Mobility Units (EMUs). These suits are customized for each astronaut and for the task that he or she must perform. Not only do they provide oxygen and proper air pressure, but they also protect astronauts from the extreme temperatures, radiation, and small particles of rock and dust found in space.

still an hour to wait before the launch. Because the shuttle stands on its end in the launch tower, Sally and the others lay on their backs waiting for the final countdown. The wait felt much longer than an hour to the excited astronauts.

Finally, the rocket boosters ignited and the shuttle blasted off, shaking ferociously and pressing the astronauts into their seats. At first, the roar from the engines was all that Sally could hear. She remembers, "For an instant, I wonder[ed] if everything [was] working right. But there's no

Sally monitors control panels on the flight deck during a shuttle mission. A flight procedures notebook floats in front of her.

Since Sally Ride made her historic flight, more than fifty women have followed in her footsteps on NASA flights.

more time to wonder, and no time to be scared."

After a few minutes, the shaking and rattling stopped, but the ride was still uncomfortable. Sally was pushed into her seat by a force that was three times stronger than the usual force of gravity. It was almost impossible to speak or move. Although she had experienced this feeling in simulators during her training, it had never lasted as long as this.

Finally, after about ten minutes, the shuttle reached its orbit. For the next six days, it circled 200 miles (322 km) above Earth's surface, with the planet filling its windows. Although Sally could not see the entire planet at once, the view was still impressive. "When I wasn't working, I was usually looking down at Earth," she remembers.

Once the shuttle reached its orbit, everything inside became weightless. Other names for weightlessness are freefall, zero-G, zero gravity, and microgravity. Despite some of its names, weightlessness isn't caused by a lack of gravity. Earth's gravity actually holds the shuttle in its orbit. As the shuttle circles Earth, it is really "falling," but the shuttle travels so fast that instead of falling to Earth, it falls around the planet. Because everything and everyone inside the shuttle is falling along with it, they become weightless. Objects float freely unless they are firmly attached to some surface. The shuttle has plenty of handholds, footholds, and Velcro straps to hold the astronauts and their gear in place.

It takes a while to get used to the feeling of weightlessness, and many astronauts suffer from nausea and headaches, known as "space sickness," for the first couple of days. Sally was one of the lucky astronauts who don't experience space sickness, so she got to enjoy weightlessness right away. "It feels wonderful to be able to float without effort," she says.

Floating may have felt wonderful, but getting around the shuttle took some work. Sally tried to move by "swimming" through the air, but she felt silly waving her arms and legs around. She soon discovered that she could move around the shuttle by pushing herself off things. But there were still problems with this method. "At first, I would push off a little too hard and crash into the opposite wall," Sally recalls. With a little practice, Sally got the hang of moving around and could even do somersaults through the air.

Sally performs her tasks in the shuttle's weightless environment.

Eating was also a challenge. Most of the food that the astronauts brought with them was sticky so that it wouldn't float away as they tried to put it into their mouths. Liquids were stored in plastic pouches and drunk through straws with clamps. Sometimes though, food would still fly—on purpose. "We set a cookie floating in the middle of the room," Sally says, "and then 'flew' an astronaut, with his mouth wide open, across the cabin to capture it."

After spending six days in space and successfully completing all of her tasks, it was time to go home. Sally stowed her equipment and put on her flight suit, boots, helmet, and life vest. She had been moving freely around the cabin, but now she had to strap herself into her seat. The ride home was about to begin.

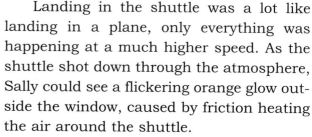

NASA space flights are named with the abbreviation "STS," which stands for "space transportation system." It refers to the entire shuttle fleet and its facilities.

Landing in the shuttle was a lot like landing in a plane, only everything was happening at a much higher speed. As the shuttle shot down through the atmosphere, Sally could see a flickering orange glow outside the window, caused by friction heating the air around the shuttle.

After the shuttle made it safely to the ground, Sally and the crew remained inside for a while. Having felt weightless for nearly a week, their bodies needed some time to readjust to the feeling of gravity. Their bodies suddenly felt so heavy that it was difficult even to walk. Once Sally had adjusted to being back on Earth, she was interviewed by NASA officials and then began a series of press conferences

Kathryn Sullivan (left) and Sally show the springs and clips used as a sleep restraint system for astronauts aboard a shuttle.

and interviews. She was a national hero. Of her experience, Sally said, "The thing I'll remember most about the flight is that it was fun. In fact, I'm sure it was the most fun that I'll ever have in my life."

A high school teacher named Christa McAuliffe was one of the astronauts aboard *Challenger* when it exploded. Christa was the first civilian ever to fly on a NASA mission. She had planned to teach two lessons from space.

Sally's flight was not only fun; it was also an important achievement for her and for millions of other people. "I did feel a special responsibility to be the first American woman in space. I felt very honored," she says. She was watched by people who were curious to see how well a woman would perform as an astronaut and by people who looked up to her as a role model. "It was very, very important that I do a good job," Sally says.

Sally received a second mission the next year. Flight STS 41-G launched on October 5, 1984. This time, Sally flew with one of her friends, Dr. Kathryn Sullivan. The two women had known each other since grade school. During this flight, Kathryn became the first American woman to perform an extra-vehicular activity (EVA), or space walk. Although Sally stayed inside the shuttle, it was exciting to see a good friend perform another important "first."

After she got back to Earth, Sally was assigned a third flight. Before her launch date, however, disaster struck the space shuttle program. On January 28, 1986, the space shuttle *Challenger* exploded minutes after its launch. Sally was shocked. What had caused this accident? How could space travel be made safer? NASA appointed Sally to a commission to investigate the accident and find answers to these questions.

The commission learned that a faulty rubber seal on the shuttle's solid rocket boosters had frozen the night before

Challenger's launch. When the rocket boosters ignited, the flames got past the seal and reached an external fuel tank, eventually leading to the explosion. The commission determined that NASA needed to be more careful about safety.

Sally prepared a report, often called the "Ride Report," to help NASA get over the blow of the *Challenger* accident. The report suggested space-exploration goals for NASA and suggested the future path of the space program. NASA's administrator told Sally, "You have contributed strongly to a process that will determine the goals and directions of the nation's civil space activities well into the next century."

In 1987, Sally retired from NASA. She joined the Center for International Security and Arms Control at Stanford University. Two years later, she became the director of the California Space Institute at the University of California, San Diego. There, Sally returned to her scientific research and became a professor, another of her goals in life. Sally also founded a group called Imaginary Lines to help encourage girls who are interested in science, math, and technology to pursue their goals. She decided to take a leave of absence from the University of California so that she could devote herself full-time to this case. She is now the president and CEO of a company called Sally Ride Science that creates programming for elementary schools that helps kids get excited about learning science.

Even though Sally is no longer an astronaut, she still loves space. She just loves what she does now more. "I would like to go back into space again," she says, "but not if it meant I had to give up the job I have now."

Chapter 5

Roberta Bondar

1945–

When Roberta Bondar was young, she and her older sister, Barbara, would explore their neighborhood, pretending they were astronauts discovering an unknown planet. Every ordinary tree, street sign, and patch of grass had to be carefully examined and studied. Just walking down the street was an adventure. As an adult, Roberta hasn't lost her sense of adventure or curiosity, although now her travels take her much farther than the edges of her neighborhood.

Roberta Lynn Bondar was born in Sault Ste. Marie, Ontario, on December 4, 1945. Her father was an office manager for the city and her mother was a teacher. They enjoyed spending time outdoors and instilled a love and respect for nature in their daughters. Camping and canoeing were some of the family's favorite pastimes.

It seems like Roberta was destined to become an astronaut. As a child, she spent hours building model rockets, space stations, and satellites and used her radio set to try to contact aliens in outer space. Roberta loved to read adventure and science-fiction books, imagining herself in the characters' places. She dreamed of traveling to space someday to see what Earth and the other planets looked like from there. Roberta also loved experimenting with her chemistry set. She enjoyed science and experimenting so much that her father built a laboratory in their basement.

During high school, Roberta continued her passion for science in and out of the classroom. For six years, Roberta spent her summer vacations working for the Department of Fisheries and Forestry, studying an insect called the spruce budworm. Spruce budworms eat coniferous trees, and they can cause a lot of damage if their population gets out of control. Through this summer job, Roberta developed a love of biology that guided her through university.

At the University of Guelph, Roberta studied agriculture (the study of farming) and zoology (the study of animals). After graduating in 1968, she went on to the University of Western Ontario, where she earned a master's degree in experimental pathology (the study of diseases), and then to the University of Toronto, where she received a doctorate in neurobiology (the biology of the brain and nervous system). After completing these degrees, Roberta studied medicine at McMaster University and became a medical doctor in 1977.

Roberta then began working as a neurologist, researching how blood flows in the brain and how changes in gravity can affect this flow. Roberta had managed to combine her love of biology with her love of space. Although she was working in the field of space medicine, actually performing her research in space didn't seem possible. No Canadian had ever been an astronaut before. But that changed when NASA offered to let Canadians join two of its missions in 1983. Almost instantly, the Canadian astronaut program was born.

Roberta and 4,000 other people applied to the National Research Council and spent the next few months waiting to find out if they'd been accepted. Roberta's good health and her scientific experience set her apart from the piles of applications that officials had to sort through. After making it through the first cuts, Roberta tackled rounds of interviews and tests. Finally, in December of 1983, Roberta learned that she and only five other people had been accepted in Canada's first astronaut program. After spending some time adjusting to the news and making arrangements to leave her job and home, Roberta reported for training in Ottawa in February 1984.

Roberta enjoyed most of the training, which involved scuba diving, riding in flight simulators, and practicing ways to escape from the shuttle. What Roberta didn't enjoy was the hectic and unpredictable schedule. It was frustrating not being able to see the people she cared about. "You'd ask ahead of time for time off," she says, "and they'd say, 'Oh yeah, definitely we're going to have this week off.' So you tell your family and friends we're going to have this big barbecue at the cottage, only to find out that that's been

Space medicine is concerned with the effects of space on the mind and body. Except for space motion sickness, short flights don't have much of an effect on astronauts' bodies. When astronauts spend weeks, or even months, in space, though, problems can develop. One problem is that bones and muscles, including the heart, become weaker. Usually these effects reverse themselves within a few weeks after astronauts return to Earth.

The first group of Canadian astronauts consisted of Roberta Bondar, Marc Garneau, Steve MacLean, Ken Money, Bob Thirsk, and Bjarni Tryggvason. Marc Garneau became the first Canadian in space in 1986.

The Canadian Space Agency was formed in 1989, five years after the first Canadian astronauts began training.

changed and you're not going to be up that week." Still, Roberta felt that the sacrifices were worth it and decided to continue training to achieve her dream of reaching space.

Roberta began to question her dream in 1986, though, when *Challenger* exploded seconds after liftoff. Although people had always known that going to space was dangerous, this accident was a harsh reminder of the risks. Some people questioned if going to space was worth the lives of the astronauts. The future of space flight was up in the air for NASA and for Roberta. She thought carefully about whether she still wanted to be an astronaut. She finally decided that, although there were risks, she was willing to face them. More than anything, she was an adventurer, and what's an adventure without danger?

The only problem that remained was whether Roberta would find an opportunity to go to space. NASA was pulling back on its plans for space flight. Although it still owed the Canadian Space Agency one more mission, NASA was in no hurry to resume its flights. After years of training, Roberta had no idea when, or if, her dream would happen. The Russian Space Agency offered Roberta the chance to join a mission to its space station, Mir, to study the effects of weightlessness on women. The offer was tempting, but in the end, Roberta declined. If she went with the Russians, she would be a test subject rather than one of the scientists conducting the experiments. Roberta decided to wait for an opportunity that would put her scientific background and abilities to use.

In the meantime, Roberta went back to her research. She studied blood flow in the brain and how it changes in low gravity. Some of her experiments were done in the KC-135 aircraft. This plane, nicknamed the "vomit comet," flies in a pattern of steep climbs and rapid dives. Every time it swoops down, everything inside it becomes weightless for about twenty to thirty seconds. It allowed Roberta to experience microgravity without going into space.

In 1990, Roberta finally got the news that she'd been waiting years to hear—she was going to make a flight on the space shuttle. She'd be able to study space science in space! On January 22, 1992, nine years after joining the astronaut program, Roberta Bondar became the first Canadian woman and the first neurologist in space. Roberta served as a payload specialist on her mission. Payload specialists are usually professional scientists. They run experiments aboard the shuttle.

Roberta conducts a life sciences experiment, studying the effects of weightlessness on small organisms during the first International Microgravity Laboratory mission.

Roberta's mission, STS-42, was also the first time the International Microgravity Laboratory was used. On this flight, it was used to study the effects of weightlessness on shrimp eggs, lentil seedlings, fruit fly eggs, and bacteria. Other experiments determined how low gravity affects the way crystals grow. The astronauts themselves were part of microgravity experiments that looked at how the human nervous system adapts to space. Roberta got to conduct an experiment that she had designed to measure blood flow in the brains of the astronauts.

The mission was supposed to last ten days, but in the end, the crew had only eight days to complete the forty-two experiments that had been planned. This tight schedule meant that the entire crew, even those crewmembers who wouldn't normally participate in scientific experiments, had

Roberta (left) and another astronaut, Steve Oswald, work in the International Microgravity Laboratory.

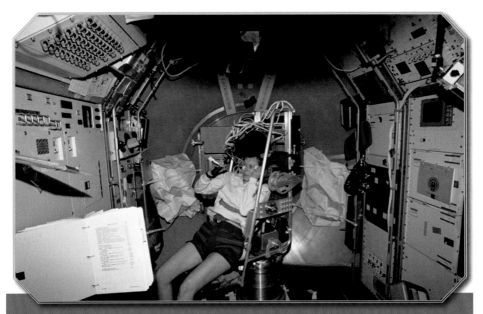

Roberta climbs into the Microgravity Vestibular Investigation chair so that her visual and vestibular (balance-related) responses to head and body movements can be monitored by the International Microgravity Laboratory.

to work around the clock to get everything done. They took turns working twelve-hour shifts. "I was lucky enough to get the day shift," Roberta says, "and my family didn't have to stay up to see us on television."

Like other astronauts, Roberta had fun with weightlessness, doing somersaults in midair and "walking" on the ceiling, but she quickly learned that it has its drawbacks, too. Everything from food to clothes to garbage would bump into the astronauts without warning. They had to spend a lot of time securing items before they could even begin their work on experiments and other tasks. "We need flypaper up there," she joked, "We need one of those creatures from *Star Wars* who gobbles the trash."

Although the busy schedule meant that the astronauts didn't have a lot of free time, Roberta still managed to enjoy the view from the shuttle's windows. "I remember the commander trying to haul me out of the flight deck to get me to sleep," she says. Looking at our planet, she remembered why she wanted to travel to space in the first place. Itwasn't just because of the science or the thrill of the experience. It was to "be somewhere and go somewhere with my mind and my head." She had traveled 188 miles (303 km) above Earth, but the greatest journey was inside herself.

After her mission, Roberta left the space program. Nine years was long enough to be an astronaut, she decided, and there were many other things that she wanted to accomplish. She became a full-time researcher again, heading an international medical team at the University of New Mexico. The team was particularly interested in learning more about the changes that occur to humans when they've been in space for a long time. Roberta also wrote a book, called *Touching the Earth*, about her experience in space.

Seeing the huge expanse of space around Earth had made Roberta realize just how small and fragile our planet is. She also realized how little of it she had seen up close. She assigned herself a new mission: She would travel

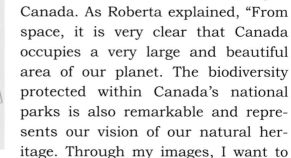

Roberta has received many honors, including the Order of Canada, the NASA Space Medal, and twenty-two honorary degrees from universities. She is also part of the Canadian Medical Hall of Fame.

around the world, taking pictures of the natural environment. Photography became her new passion. Her first goal was to document the natural beauty of Canada. As Roberta explained, "From space, it is very clear that Canada occupies a very large and beautiful area of our planet. The biodiversity protected within Canada's national parks is also remarkable and represents our vision of our natural heritage. Through my images, I want to share my passion, admiration, and deep respect for this part of the planet—our Canada." Roberta spent two years traveling across the country and photographing all forty-one of its national parks. She collected her photographs into a book and touring exhibit called *Passionate Vision: Discovering Canada's National Parks*. Roberta hopes that they will inspire people to want to preserve and protect the environment.

Roberta's many accomplishments have earned her a great deal of respect, which has given her the power to speak out about issues that are important to her, such as the environment. She hopes that by sharing what she has seen, from her travels both in space and on Earth, she can encourage others to become more aware of how delicate the planet is. "Although I cared deeply about the environment before I flew in space, I became passionate about it during my flight. My sense of responsibility reaches beyond my lifetime to the future generations of the planet," she says.

Roberta has left quite a legacy. There are now a number of Canadian schools that bear her name. In 2011, it was announced that she would be inducted into Canada's Walk of Fame. Roberta has no plans to make a second trip into space. When she flew aboard *Discovery* in 1992, it seemed like the greatest adventure she could have. It turned out to be just the beginning of an even bigger one. Roberta is determined to learn as much as she can about the world, and the universe, in which she lives. No doubt, she'll do it with the curiosity and courage that have taken her to space and back.

Chapter 6

Ellen Ochoa

1958–

On July 20, 1969, millions of people gathered around their television sets to watch Neil Armstrong become the first person to walk on the moon. Eleven-year-old Ellen Ochoa was one of them. At the time, it didn't occur to Ellen that she could be an astronaut someday. The only astronauts at that time were men. It wasn't until 1983, when Sally Ride became the first American woman in space, that Ellen decided to become an astronaut. Ellen is now famous for being the first Hispanic female astronaut.

Ellen was born on May 10, 1958, in Los Angeles, California, but she grew up down the coast in La Mesa, California. Ellen lived there with her mother, her sister, and three brothers. Her parents separated when Ellen was in junior high school.

Ellen's father's parents moved to the United States from Mexico before he was born, and he grew up speaking both Spanish and English. Ellen did not learn Spanish at home, though. As she explains, "When I was growing up, my father believed as many people did at the time that there was a prejudice against people speaking their native language. It's really too bad, and I'm glad that things have changed in recent years."

Ellen's mother, Rosanne, placed a lot of importance on learning and education, both for her children and for herself. She began taking university courses when Ellen was one year old. As a single parent, Rosanne didn't have a lot of time for school between raising her five children and working, but she managed to take one class each semester. No matter how difficult it became trying to balance her family and her education, Rosanne never lost patience and she never gave up. After more than twenty years of attending university, Rosanne graduated with three degrees.

Rosanne's dedication to her education inspired Ellen to study hard. Ellen's favorite subject was math, which she used to earn a degree in physics from the University of San Diego in 1980. She then went to Stanford University, where she earned two more degrees in electrical engineering.

Although Ellen's formal education focused on science, she was also interested in music. As a girl, Ellen had earned recognition for playing the flute, and she wanted to make sure music was always part of her life. She continued to perform and earn awards in university as a soloist in the Stanford Symphony Orchestra.

NASA Facilities

NASA has many centers all over the United States where it conducts research and test new equipment and spacecraft. The agency's headquarters are in Washington, D.C., but much of the work for space flight is done at the Johnson Space Center in Texas. This is where astronauts train and where mission control is located. Shuttles are launched at the Kennedy Space Center in Cape Canaveral, Florida.

After earning her Ph.D. in 1985, Ellen applied for NASA's astronaut program but was not selected. Ellen began working as a researcher at Sandia National Laboratories in New Mexico, and later, at NASA's Ames Research Center in California. She continued research, which was focused on optics, that she had started in university. Optics is the science of vision and light, and it includes instruments, such as lenses, that are used for seeing. Whenever you use a microscope, telescope, camera, or your own eyes, you are using optics. Ellen designed ways of using computers to "see" things and to make conclusions about what they see.

Ellen designed three new inventions while she worked as a researcher. One invention is a computer system that is able to inspect objects and detect problems in equipment. Another is a system that can "recognize" objects. The other invention is a computer system that can make images clearer. All of them have the potential to be used for exploring space.

While she worked as a researcher, Ellen continued to dream about becoming an astronaut. Although her first

There were no female or Hispanic astronauts when Ellen was growing up. At the time, there were no African-American astronauts either. Mae Jemison, who became the first African-American woman in space in 1992, looked up to the only female and African-American astronaut she knew of—Lieutenant Uhura on the TV show *Star Trek*. Today, Mae and Ellen provide real-life inspiration for girls of all backgrounds, and have set important examples for African-American and Hispanic girls.

application to NASA's astronaut program had been rejected, Ellen didn't give up. Instead, she worked on gaining the skills and experience she knew NASA looked for so that she'd have a better shot at being accepted the next time she applied. In her spare time, she earned her pilot's license. "That's very important—not giving up," she says. "It definitely is one of those jobs where you can increase your skills and career achievements, and continue to reapply." In 1990, Ellen's determination paid off. She was accepted into the astronaut training program. A year later, she became an official NASA astronaut.

"I can only imagine the amazement and pride my grandparents would feel, having been born in Mexico in the 1870s, on knowing that their granddaughter grew up to travel in space. Their move to the United States to raise their family, along with my mother's passion for learning, provided me with the opportunity and motivation to get an education and set high goals."

Ellen's first trip into space was on Mission STS-56 aboard the shuttle *Discovery* in April of 1993. Ellen was a mission specialist on this flight. A mission specialist is an astronaut who conducts experiments, uses the robotic arm, or does a space walk. Ellen's most exciting task during this mission was to fly the Shuttle Remote Manipulator System (SRMS), or the Canadarm, to deploy a satellite from the shuttle's cargo area, or payload bay. The satellite, called SPARTAN-201, traveled behind the shuttle as it orbited Earth, collecting information about the sun. Two days later, Ellen used the arm again to grab onto SPARTAN-201 and pull it back into the payload bay.

In November 1994, Ellen flew her second mission. This time, she flew aboard the space shuttle *Atlantis* and served as the mission's payload commander. The payload is whatever cargo the shuttle carries that isn't part of its regular operation. A payload could be a satellite, supplies to conduct

Ellen positions a camera on the flight deck of Discovery.

experiments, or supplies or equipment to be delivered to a space station. On her mission, Ellen was responsible for picking up the cargo, a satellite that had to be retrieved from orbit and returned to Earth. Ellen again used the robotic arm to carry out her task.

Ellen's third mission, STS-96, was a historic flight. It was the first time a space shuttle docked, or joined up with, the International Space Station (ISS). Construction of the station had begun the year before, in 1998, with the launch of the first two sections, or modules. The purpose of STS-96 was to deliver supplies such as clothing, sleeping bags, medical equipment, spare parts, and water to prepare the station for astronauts to live aboard. The crew also did some maintenance work on the newly built station.

Ellen served as both a mission specialist and a flight engineer. A flight engineer is in charge of the mechanical operation of the shuttle in flight. As the mission specialist, she operated the shuttle's robotic arm. Unlike the other times she'd used the arm, this time Ellen didn't grab satellites with it. Instead, she used the arm to help her crewmate Terry Jernigan perform space walks around the outside of the station to complete construction jobs. Terry held on to a piece of equipment and Ellen used the arm to move her to the work site. Because she was moving Terry to various parts of the station, Ellen couldn't always see her and the arm through the shuttle's window.

The Shuttle Remote Manipulator System (SRMS), or Canadarm, is controlled by two levers that are like joysticks. One moves the arm up and down, and the other moves it from side to side. A separate control allows the arm to grab or release objects. Astronauts need steady hands and excellent coordination to control the arm.

Instead, she had to depend on cameras and computer tools to make sure that she was moving the arm to exactly the right spot. It was a real test of her hand-eye coordination!

Ellen's most recent trip to the International Space Station was in 2002 as part of Mission STS-110. Ellen found that the ISS was very different from the last time she had visited. It was much larger, and there was a crew living aboard it full time. The goal of Mission STS-110 was to continue the ISS's construction by adding a new section of the truss. The truss is a metal framework that is like the ISS's backbone. Solar panels, labs, living quarters, and other parts of the ISS are connected to it. The truss also supports the Mobile Transporter, which Ellen and her crewmates delivered. The Mobile Transporter is like a railway car that slides along tracks on the outside of the station. It is used to move the ISS's robotic arm, known as Canadarm2, from one end of the station to the other.

Ellen and her crewmates installed the truss and Mobile Transporter during four long space walks. Ellen used the

Ellen looks through the window of the International Space Station, viewing portions of the Canadarm2 (bottom of the window, horizontal) and the space shuttle Atlantis (sticking out behind the Canadarm2).

shuttle's arm to maneuver the huge pieces out of the shuttle's payload bay and into place. Astronauts worked outside of the station to connect the new sections. Ellen and two other astronauts used the Canadarm2—the first time it was used—to move the astronauts from one work site to another to complete the construction. A camera on the arm allowed people inside the station and on Earth to see what was happening as the astronauts worked.

Although the main reason for *Atlantis* to dock with the ISS was to continue the station's construction, the mission offered a bonus to the three astronauts who had been living there for months—fresh faces! Ellen and her crewmates enjoyed sharing meals and stories with them before returning to Earth.

Astronauts Yvonne Cagle, left, and Ellen, right, participate in a women's forum on space. At center is Jennifer Harris, system manager at the Jet Propulsion Laboratory.

As of 2004, Ellen had spent over 978 hours in space. Since her mission in 2002, Ellen has remained an active astronaut. Like most astronauts, she is expected to help out on a variety of projects on the ground. She has worked on flight software, developed and tested robotics systems and taught others to use them, and served as a CAPCOM at mission control. Ellen has also been Assistant for the Space

Ellen holds her son, Wilson, following her return from a third space shuttle mission.

Station to the Chief of the Astronaut Office and the Acting Deputy Chief of the Astronaut Office. In addition to her duties at NASA, Ellen also spends time traveling to schools to speak with students, telling them about the types of careers they can have if they study science. She believes that it is important for them to realize all the opportunities there are. She says, "The key is learning more about what jobs are available out there, what kinds of things you do when you are on the job, and what kind of education you need in order to get those jobs."

Besides being an astronaut, Ellen is also a wife and mother. It can be challenging balancing her job and her family. As Ellen says, "This career takes a lot of time, and you need to travel a lot. You often have strange hours, because it's not a regular schedule, so childcare is an issue. A lot of astronaut women face that." Still, she's happy with her career choice. While she may try something new in the future, right now she loves what she does.

Chapter 7

Eileen Collins
1956-

Traveling into space can be an incredibly dangerous and difficult experience. However, pushing beyond the boundaries of what women are allowed to do is just as important as rocketing past the limits of Earth's atmosphere. Eileen Collins was at the forefront of women's participation in the space program. She was always perfectly comfortable being a pioneer, and she paved new ground as naturally, skillfully, and gracefully as she piloted and commanded enormous shuttles through space.

Eileen was born on November 19, 1956, in Elmira, New York. Elmira was a fitting place for someone whose future would take them high into the skies since it's known as the "soaring capital" of the United States. The city earned this title because it is the home of the Harris Hills Soaring Center, where pilots of gliders (airplanes without engines) gather to fly. The city also has a rich history in flight, beginning in the late 1890s. Growing up in Elmira, Eileen's earliest memories are of watching the planes take off while sitting on the hood of her father's car. One day at summer camp in Elmira, after a day spent watching the gliders peacefully soaring in the clear blue sky above her, Eileen determined that her dream to fly would one day become a reality.

Unfortunately for Eileen, achieving this dream would not come easily. When Eileen was nine-years-old, her parents separated. Her father, Jack Collins, lost his job at the post office, and her mother, Rose, had trouble finding a job. For a time, Eileen and her three brothers lived with their mother in low-income housing and survived on food stamps. The family's financial situation improved when Eileen's father got a job as a surveyor and her mother found work in a nearby prison, but there was still little room for luxuries in the Collins household. Eileen really wanted to take flying lessons, but her parents couldn't afford to pay for them, or even a ride in a plane. Eileen refused to let that stand in her way. She turned to books and read everything she could about airplanes, from the earliest gliders made by the Wright Brothers to fighter planes used during World Wars I and II. During her high school years, she worked nights in a pizza parlor to save up the $1,000 she needed for flying lessons. At age nineteen, she finally saved enough money and climbed into her very first plane. She never looked back. From that moment on, Eileen knew she would be a professional pilot.

Eileen worked her way through Corning Community College in New York in 1974, earning an associate's degree in mathematics. She was awarded a scholarship that allowed her to go to Syracuse University and receive a bachelor's degree in mathematics and economics in 1978. Eileen refused to believe the idea that only men could fly jets. She began a training program with the Air Force in 1978 at the Vance Air Force Base in Oklahoma. This was the same year that the National Aeronautics and Space Administration (NASA) opened the space shuttle program to women. Through her program with the Air Force, she learned how to be a military fighter pilot. This training program had only recently been opened to female pilots. Collins was one of four women chosen for the program. The rest of her classmates, in a class of 320, were all men. After a year of training, Eileen became the first female in U.S. Air Force history to become a flight instructor.

Eileen continued to be a flight instructor until 1990. She taught at air bases from Oklahoma to California. During the time she was a teacher, she continued to be a student as well. She earned a master's of science degree in operations research from Stanford University in California, in 1986. She then went on to earn a master's of arts degree in space systems management from Webster University in St. Louis, Missouri, in 1989. By 1989, Eileen had logged in a whopping 1,500 hours of flight time and earned herself several advanced degrees. In 1989, she became only the second woman ever to be accepted to the prestigious Air Force Test Pilot School at Edwards Air Force Base in California.

While there she held her own in the male-dominated ranks of the military and cemented a reputation for being a cool, levelheaded pilot. It came as no surprise, then, that when Eileen graduated from the program in 1990, she was a hot commodity. NASA handpicked her to join its program, and she began training to become an astronaut.

Becoming an astronaut is no walk in the park. Eileen had to take many classes on survival and parachute training.

She also had to learn about the history of the space program, as well as things that can affect a space shuttle launch, landing, and operations like weather and mechanics. But by far the most difficult part of astronaut training is the simulations. NASA has many high-tech simulators that recreate the experience of a real space shuttle launch without a trainee ever having to leave the ground. During these sessions, which lasted around eight minutes each, instructors make things go wrong so that the trainees would learn to be ready for any possible malfunction that could take place during a mission. Eileen had to learn to make life-and-death decisions in mere seconds.

In 1991, Eileen was officially an astronaut with NASA. However, she didn't go on a shuttle mission right away. For four years, Eileen worked on the ground, offering technical support. She served as a Spacecraft Communicator, meaning she talked to people in space while at mission control. She also served in several leadership positions at NASA, from the Branch Chief of the Astronaut Office Spacecraft Systems to the Branch Chief of Astronaut Safety. After all these roles and experiences, Eileen was fully prepared to take on her own shuttle mission. And in 1995, she got her chance— NASA selected her as a space shuttle pilot.

Eileen's first shuttle mission was part of a new collaborative space program created by the United States and Russia. Eileen was in charge of piloting the U.S. shuttle *Discovery* to the Russia's Mir space station. She was excited to finally get to put all of her training into action. After the roar of the engines and the eight-and-a-half minute launch—this time not a simulation—Eileen took out a pen and saw it was floating because of the zero gravity. She was finally in space!

This was a monumental occasion, not only for Eileen, but for the space program as a whole and for women everywhere. Eileen was the first woman ever to pilot a space shuttle. On her return to Earth, she was awarded the Harmon Trophy. The Harmon Trophy is an award given out each year to people who have made great achievements in space flight. However, Eileen wasn't content to go to space just once—she was itching to go back. In 1997, she got her chance when she was selected to pilot a second *Discovery* mission to the Mir space station.

Eileen suits up and prepares for blastoff.

Then in 1999, Eileen made history again when she became the first woman to command a space shuttle mission. This is an even more important job than piloting the ship. She was in charge of making sure everyone on board was safe and the mission was accomplished smoothly. Her assignment was to command a five-person crew on the space shuttle *Columbia*. The flight's primary mission was to launch a huge X-ray telescope. The Chandra X-Ray Observatory, as the telescope was called, would be used to help people on Earth learn more about space and very distant objects and celestial bodies.

With space missions, there are always surprises. The *Columbia* mission did not start off without a hitch. During the launch, some bad wiring on the shuttle caused two of the shuttle's three engines to fail. Luckily, *Columbia* had back-up engines that kicked in, but the trouble was not over yet. Another problem surfaced when a fuel line started leaking. Eileen remained cool under pressure throughout it all. Despite all the problems, she was able to guide the crew through launch, the five-day mission, and a safe landing.

As the 1999 *Columbia* mission showed, no matter how many precautions are taken, space travel is still dangerous and things can always go wrong. In 2003, the space shuttle *Columbia* again went into space, although this time Eileen was watching from the ground. Underestimated damage to the shuttle's heat-absorbing wing tiles during launch caused the ship to explode on re-entry into Earth's atmosphere. The loss of the *Columbia* and its brave crew members was a huge blow to the U.S. space program. It was this tragic disaster that caused Eileen to take on what was arguably her most important mission.

In 2005, Eileen agreed to pilot the space shuttle *Discovery* on a fourteen-day mission to improve safety features for future shuttle missions. It was also intended to restore people's confidence in the space program. One of the most important aspects of the *Discovery* mission was to do the first-ever nose-over-tail spin after launch. The reason for this new precaution was so that the entire shuttle could be photographed and inspected for damage after launch. This way the people in charge of the mission on the ground could make sure that what occurred in the 2003 *Columbia* explosion would not happen again. Always the skilled pilot, Eileen was up to the challenge. She was not scared for her safety, but focused on the mission and what it would mean for the future of manned space flight. On August 10, 2005, after a successful fourteen-day mission, Eileen piloted the *Discovery* safely back to Earth at Edward's Air Force Base.

Today, Eileen lives with her husband and two daughters in California. In her hometown of Elmira, New

York, she is truly a celebrity. The Eileen Collins Observatory was established at the Corning Community College, where Eileen got her first degree. She has also been honored with many awards for her achievements, including the NASA Outstanding Leadership Medal and the Distinguished Flying Cross. She has also been inducted into the National Women's Hall of Fame in Seneca Falls, New York. In 2006, Eileen decided to retire from space flight. Although she will not again slip the bonds of our planet and its atmosphere, Eileen has certainly left her mark, both on Earth and far, far beyond.

Julie Payette

1963–

"Our crew motto was, 'If you're not having fun, you're not doing it right.' I don't know if we did it right, but we sure had fun," Julie Payette has said about her mission to space. Don't be fooled by this laid-back attitude, though. Julie is intensely passionate and serious about being the Chief Astronaut for the Canadian Space Agency. She has even called herself a perfectionist when it comes to her work. She knows it's important to love what you do, and having fun is one of the reasons why she says being an astronaut is the best job on Earth.

Julie was born on October 20, 1963, in Montreal, Quebec. She grew up in a Montreal suburb with her older brother, Simon, and her younger sister, Maude. As a child, she watched the Apollo missions on television, read about them in magazines, and became obsessed with everything that had to do with space. She loved the space suits, the lunar vehicles, and the astronauts. She even had a picture of Neil Armstrong pinned up on her bedroom wall.

Although she dreamed of exploring space, it was a dream that seemed unlikely to come true. "You can imagine," Julie says, "that when you are ten, twelve years old and you're growing up in a town in Canada and you're French Canadian and you're telling everybody, 'Hey, I'd like to be an astronaut one day.' Then people pat you on the back, smile a bit, and say, 'Yeah, sure.' And they hope that you're going to change your mind and find a more down-to-earth job."

At the time when Julie was growing up, Canada didn't have a space program. Only the United States and the Soviet Union (later Russia) were sending people into space. Still, Julie held on to her dream. She did well in school, both in science and in the arts, and impressed her teachers with her hard work and friendly nature.

When she was sixteen years old, Julie received a scholarship to the United World International College of the Atlantic in South Wales. She was one of only six Canadian students who were accepted that year. The college brings together high school–age students from all over the world in order to increase international understanding. It gave Julie the opportunity to travel, live in a new place, and meet new people. Her experience at the school helped to make her the person she is today. She says, "I am still driven by the ideals of the college: dedication to learning, understanding between nations, and commitment to community service."

After two years at Atlantic College, Julie returned to Canada to continue her education. She studied computer engineering at McGill University in Montreal and at the University of Toronto.

Before applying to become an astronaut, Julie worked in the computer industry developing ways of making computers understand human speech. Talking is easy for most of us, so we rarely think about the many steps that are involved when we have a conversation. We open our mouths, the words come out, and we understand what they mean. For computers, though, it is much more difficult. They need to be programmed to recognize every small part of language and know how it works.

Julie's education may have focused on computers and engineering, but her interests have always gone far beyond these fields. One of her passions is music. Some people may think that art and science are conflicting interests, but Julie is proof that a person can make room for both of them in her life. She not only plays the piano and flute, she's also an accomplished singer. While she was in university and, later, working, she performed with world-class choirs: the Montreal Symphonic Orchestra Chamber Choir, the Piacere Vocale in Switzerland, and the Tafelmusik Baroque Orchestra Choir in Toronto.

Before the International Space Station, the oldest space station orbiting the Earth was Mir. First built by the Soviet Union in 1986, Mir was expanded many times before it was taken out of orbit in 2001. The United States also had a space station, called Skylab. It was in orbit from 1973 to 1979.

Although her music and her work kept her busy, Julie didn't forget about her dream to become an astronaut. In 1992, the Canadian Space Agency (CSA) advertised that it was accepting applications. This was only the second time that the CSA had recruited new astronauts, so Julie jumped at the opportunity.

The application and screening process took months. During one interview, Julie was asked about how she works in teams. She told the interviewer about her experience singing with choirs and explained that being in a choir requires a lot of teamwork. When she sings, she has to really listen to what others are doing. She can't just focus on her own part.

Julie would soon learn firsthand that working as part of a team is as necessary in space as it is in choirs. Of the 5,330 people who applied for the program, Julie was one of four who were selected to become astronaut candidates. Julie had to wait a little longer to get to space, though. Like all new astronauts, she had to spend time working on the ground to prepare for space flight. Julie put her engineering knowledge and experience to work for the CSA. She acted as a technical advisor on one of the CSA's biggest projects, a huge robotic arm called the Mobile Servicing System (MSS), or Canadarm2, for the International Space Station.

Julie also prepared in other ways before her first space flight. As part of her astronaut basic training, she learned how to scuba dive and parachute, and she spent 120 hours on reduced-gravity aircraft. One part of her training involved learning how to fly a jet at the Canadian Air Force Base in Moose Jaw, Saskatchewan. As with everything that she does, Julie was determined to excel at flying. She spent as much time as she could practicing and was only satisfied when she could fly as well as her instructors. Although she sometimes became frustrated as she learned to handle the jet, her mistakes just made her work harder to master this new skill. Julie practiced on as many flights as she could.

The International Space Station

Sixteen countries worked together to build the International Space Station (ISS). It is the largest structure ever built in space, with a mass of 470 tons. The construction of ISS began in 1998 and took years to complete. It is used to conduct experiments in space and monitor changes in Earth's environment.

During training, Julie poses next to the Canadarm2.

Julie didn't limit her training to just the technical, scientific, and mechanical knowledge astronauts need. Knowing that the ISS is a shared project between the United States, Russia, Canada, Japan, Brazil, and eleven European countries, Julie decided to learn to speak Russian so that she'd be able to talk with cosmonauts. Today she can speak six languages: French, English, Russian, Spanish, Italian, and German. It makes working with her international colleagues much easier—and more fun!

In 1996, Julie finished her basic training in Canada and went to NASA's Johnson Space Center in Houston, Texas, to complete her training and prepare for space flight. She had to be away from her husband, Francois Brisette, and the rest of her family, but she wasn't lonely because she found herself surrounded by others who shared her dream of space flight.

Julie was the first person from her graduating class at NASA to receive a flight assignment. It was so soon after graduation that she was far from expecting it. When the Chief Astronaut called her into his office to tell her the good news, she thought that she was in trouble for speeding around the space center! Receiving the assignment was a great honor for Julie, but she knew she still had a lot more to learn. "I'm thinking I better work even harder because I want to really be ready. I don't want to make a mistake," she admitted at the time.

Julie was assigned to be a mission specialist on Mission STS-96 on the space shuttle *Discovery*. This mission was one of many that helped build the International Space Station. When the first two modules of the ISS were launched in 1998, they did not have all of the equipment and supplies that astronauts would later need. Launching the modules fully supplied would have made them too heavy to reach their orbit. The crew's job on STS-96 was to dock with the modules and bring aboard supplies that would be used by future crews

Julie closes a container to be brought aboard Mission STS-96.

living on the space station. The crew delivered four tons of equipment, but that wasn't all they did. Being the first visitors to the space station meant that they had their work cut out for them!

After launching the space station modules, NASA had learned that there were glitches with some of the station's equipment. The crew had to repair and adjust the equipment before anyone would be able to live there. One of these repairs involved the life-support system. This system moves air around the station, making it possible for human beings to breathe. The system worked fine at moving the air, but its fans were too noisy. The crew installed mufflers around them, making it much easier to live and work near them.

One of Julie's responsibilities was to replace malfunctioning battery packs. Julie and fellow crewmate Valery

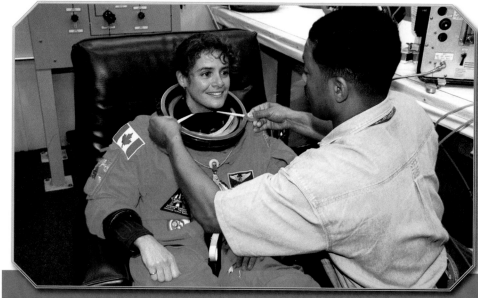

A suit technician helps Julie get into her launch and re-entry suit during final launch preparations for the mission.

Tokarev replaced eighteen units, called MIRTs, that control the charging and discharging of the station's batteries. With these units replaced, the station could use its power more effectively. Making sure that the MIRTs were replaced correctly was so important that Julie traveled to Russia beforehand to practice with Valery Tokarev in a full-scale model of the module.

Julie was also the designated "Stow Master" on the mission. Moving into the space station was a lot like moving to a new home. After everything is packed up in the old house, it has to be unpacked, sorted, and put away in the new place. Julie had to safely put away all of the equipment that they brought. She also recorded the location of each item so that future astronauts in the space station would be able to find everything.

Another of Julie's duties was to operate the shuttle's Remote Manipulator System (RMS), or Canadarm. Although the Canadarm is usually used to grab and move heavy pieces of equipment, Julie didn't use the arm to move anything. Instead, she used the camera mounted at the end of the arm to inspect the outside of the International Space Station. Julie was able to see parts of the station that she couldn't have reached otherwise. She checked areas of the station that would be worked on during future missions, making sure they were not damaged. Even a minor problem with one of the sections could throw off construction plans or endanger an astronaut working on it.

Starshine
Mission STS-96 released a small satellite as part of its assignment. The Student Tracked Atmospheric Research Satellite for Heuristic International Networking Equipment, or STARSHINE for short, was the size of a basketball and covered with mirrors. Students from schools all over the world learned about space by tracking its orbit and its eventual decay. Although it was very small, its reflective surface made STARSHINE visible from Earth.

Julie was the first Canadian aboard the International Space Station, so she made sure to bring items that, to her, represented Canada and her home province of Quebec. She brought CDs by Canadian musicians, including the Tafelmusik Baroque Orchestra Choir she had performed with. She also brought the crest of the Montreal Canadiens hockey team, a clown nose from Le Cirque du Soleil, and a bottle of maple syrup, which she shared with her crewmates.

On the ride home, Julie sat on the flight deck behind the pilot. From there, she monitored what was happening to the shuttle and had a perfect view as the shuttle neared Earth. *Discovery* landed on June 6, 1999, after spending more than nine days and nineteen hours in space. It had orbited Earth 153 times.

Since her mission, Julie has continued to work on the International Space Station. For three years, she worked on test activities for the space station in Europe and Russia

Julie talks to the media at Kennedy Space Center.

with other space agencies. Julie served for seven years as the Chief Astronaut for the Canadian Space Agency, representing the agency and coordinating activities for Canadian astronauts. Like all active-duty astronauts, she trained regularly to maintain her skills while hoping to be given another flight assignment. She also worked as a Capsule Communicator, or CAPCOM, in Houston at the Mission Control Center. A CAPCOM speaks directly with astronauts from mission control. In 2009, her wish for another space mission came true. Julie joined the crew of the space shuttle *Endeavor* as the mission specialist.

Although Julie is a very private person and does not talk much about her personal life, she is clearly enthusiastic about her work. Her sister Maude says, "She's an extremely passionate and dynamic person. She really loves what she's doing, and she also loves talking about it." According to Julie, exploring space is part of human evolution. "If we don't do it today, we'll do it tomorrow because it's part of progress; it's part of our future." The International Space Station is an important step toward being able to live in space, and Julie is thrilled to contribute to its success.

Julie may have achieved her dream of flying in space, but that doesn't mean she's stopped dreaming. "There's always a challenge, something else to do," she says. "You have to continue, always striving for that goal." Julie's a perfect example of just how much a person can achieve by following that advice.

Chiaki Mukai

1952–

M ost people think of a doctor as someone who works in a hospital, clinic, or laboratory. Few people would expect to find a doctor in space, but Chiaki Mukai is just that kind of doctor. She is both a medical doctor and an astronaut. She is also the first Japanese woman to fly in space. During her two missions she has spent over 566 hours beyond Earth's atmosphere, conducted many experiments, and represented her country in space.

Chiaki Mukai was born in 1952, in Tatebayashi, a small town in Japan. Growing up, she never dreamed of walking on the moon or flying to Mars. Chiaki says, "I realized I wanted to be an astronaut when I was thirty-two years old. Before that, in Japan, we didn't have the opportunity for people to go into space." Instead, when she was ten years old, Chiaki decided that she would be a doctor. Her younger brother had problems with his legs that caused him to walk differently from other children. He was often teased. Chiaki hated to see other children making fun of her brother. She thought that if she were a doctor, she could help him.

When she was fourteen, Chiaki moved by herself to Tokyo so that she could go to the Keio Girls High School. Although it was hard to leave her family when she was so young, she wanted the best education that she could get. After high school, Chiaki went to the Keio University and graduated from medical school in 1977.

Although her brother's medical problems had inspired her to become a doctor, Chiaki found that she was most interested in heart surgery. She did residencies, or training, at four different hospitals to gain the experience she needed to become a surgeon. While she was training, Chiaki met a doctor named Mukai Makio at Keio University Hospital in Tokyo, and they got married in 1982. Shortly after, Chiaki became the Chief Resident in Cardiovascular Surgery at Keio University Hospital and was soon promoted to Associate Professor of the university's department of Cardiovascular Surgery. Chiaki loved being a surgeon and being able to help other people. Her patients' smiles when they left the hospital were especially rewarding to her.

While reading a newspaper one day in 1983, Chiaki saw an article that changed the course of her life: Japan was looking for astronauts. The Japanese space agency was looking to train scientists as payload specialists to fly with

NASA and represent Japan in space. Payload specialists are astronauts who conduct experiments aboard a space flight. They are sometimes selected by commercial or research organizations and sometimes by governments. "Oh my God, now even a Japanese scientist can go into space," Chiaki thought. Before she read this article, she had always thought that astronauts had to be American or Russian pilots. She was interested in the

Japan's Space Agency
When Chiaki first became an astronaut, she was involved with NASDA, or the National Space Development Agency. On October 1, 2003, NASDA joined together with two other Japanese agencies to form the Japan Aerospace Exploration Agency, or JAXA. Before this time, research into space and the development of technology was divided up. Now that everyone was working together, JAXA hoped to increase its role in space exploration.

opportunity right away, and, after thinking about it for a few days, she decided to apply. "I grew more and more intrigued about personally seeing our blue planet from outer space," she says. The day she sent in her application, Chiaki began learning English and lifting weights in the hope that she would be chosen.

At the time, Chiaki says, Japan was "more of a male-dominated country." But she didn't let being a woman discourage her: "The fact that I am a woman has never occurred to me as either a limitation or advantage.... If you can dream it, you can do it." Out of the hundreds of applications, Chiaki was one of three astronaut candidates that were chosen. Only one would go to space on this mission. Mamoru Mohri, a nuclear scientist, was the lucky candidate to be selected. Chiaki was disappointed, but she told herself that her time would come eventually.

Chiaki was named as a backup crew member for the mission. If, for some reason, Mohri couldn't go on the flight, Chiaki had to be prepared to step in for him. As a backup crew member, part of her job also involved helping with the mission from the ground. Working at mission control, Chiaki saw that it took many people working together to make a mission successful. She realized that although it looks as if astronauts have the most important job, they are only one part of the team. While it was great to be any part of that team, Chiaki still dreamed of being an astronaut. She continued to train and she applied again for another mission.

In 1992, Chiaki was selected to fly and began training for her first trip to space. Chiaki spent the next two years preparing for her flight, preparations that included more than 1,000 flights aboard a microgravity plane.

Unfortunately, Chiaki found out firsthand that twenty-second bursts of weightlessness in a plane can't quite prepare a person for the experience of living in weightlessness. She suffered from space sickness the first few days she was in orbit. Chiaki took her sickness in stride, saying with her usual good humor, "I couldn't tell which [was] the ceiling and which [was] the floor. Sometimes I felt the wall or floor was my ceiling and I thought, 'Gee, that's a wonderful experience' and I wish I could see what is happening in my inner ear, my gravity-sensing organ."

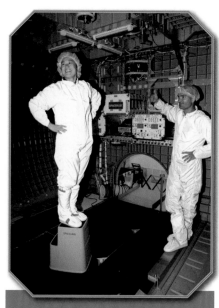

Chiaki gets a thumbs-up while familiarizing herself with the environment in which she will conduct in-flight experiments.

During the fifteen days that Chiaki and her crewmates spent in orbit, they performed eighty-two experiments in the International Microgravity Laboratory. The crew was divided into two teams to work day and night to complete the experiments, which were created by more than 200 scientists from all over the world. Scientists have a lot of questions about how microgravity affects living things, but very few scientists ever get the chance to go to space. Instead, they design experiments that astronauts do for them.

Experiments in space are carried out in the Spacelab. Built by the European Space Agency, it is made of smaller components that can be arranged differently for each mission. Because there is no up or down in space, equipment is installed on every interior surface.

Some of the experiments on STS-65 were focused on finding ways to help astronauts remain healthy during long space flights. Chiaki participated in one experiment to test a device that gets fluids to circulate through the lower body in microgravity. Astronauts have problems with circulation because when they become weightless, their blood moves up to their heads and upper bodies. Their hearts become used to pumping blood only to their upper bodies, which can become dangerous when the astronauts return home. The device that Chiaki tested is like a big sack that fits over an astronaut's legs and seals around the waist. At first, Chiaki had trouble getting a good seal around her waist because the device was too large for her. Her crewmates improvised and added some extra padding around her middle so that she would fill out the device and the experiment could be finished.

Besides being a test subject, Chiaki also carried out experiments. She studied how gravity affects plants and fish. While most of the experiments went well, microgravity threw a few unexpected glitches into some. The crew had brought cells with them to study growth hormones, but the cells clumped together during the flight. Chiaki tried to carry on with the experiment, but eventually she had to cancel it.

Chiaki loved the work that she was doing, but more than anything she was amazed by the view from the shuttle. "The Earth was so magnificent and elegant," she says. The planet looked to her as if it were wrapped in delicate white lace. She was proud that she came from such a beautiful planet.

Chiaki spent two weeks in space as part of STS-65. No female astronaut had remained in space for that long before. After returning to Earth, Chiaki had a new appreciation for gravity. "When you get back," she explains, "you feel your body is so heavy. Your body is pulled to the center of the Earth." She could even notice the weight of something as

Chiaki enters the International Microgravity Laboratory 2 spacelab science module to begin a busy twelve-hour shift to monitor the mission's experiments.

small as a business card. She recalls, "For nearly three days after touchdown, every step reminded me of gravity. Every move I made was a tussle with weight. Yet after three days, my body adjusted. Isn't that marvelous?"

In 1998, Chiaki was selected for another mission, STS-95. It gained a lot of publicity because John Glenn, the first American to orbit Earth, was going to be part of it. At seventy-seven, he was the oldest astronaut ever to fly in space. Almost forty years after his first flight, Glenn returned to orbit to participate in studies that investigated the similarities between the effects of space flight and aging on the human body. Once again, Chiaki conducted experiments that looked at the difference between being on Earth and being in space. She planted cucumbers to see if microgravity affects their growth. She examined motion sickness in fish. Along with John Glenn, she was also the subject of an experiment that studied how hormones affect an astronaut's sleep in space. Scientists were trying to figure out why most astronauts sleep poorly while in orbit.

Chiaki wanted to do more than just study life in space, though. She wanted to share the experience of being in space with others. While she was aboard the shuttle, she composed the first half of a *tanka* poem about what it feels

The animals Chiaki studied in space were part of a long line of animal space travelers. The first animal in space was a dog named Laika who traveled on *Sputnik 2* in 1957. She died after a week of orbiting Earth when her air supply ran out. The first animals to return safely from space were two monkeys, Able and Baker, who flew aboard *Jupiter* in 1959.

Naoko Sumino is Japan's newest female astronaut. She was born in 1970 in Matsudo City. She completed astronaut training in 2001, after having been an aeronautical engineer.

Chiaki is cheered on during a parade celebrating a successful mission.

like to be weightless. A tanka poem is a traditional form of Japanese poetry that is five lines long. The first and third lines have five syllables and the rest have seven syllables. Chiaki put out a call for others to finish the second half of the poem. The response was amazing—144,781 verses were submitted by poets of all ages!

Chiaki is still active in the space program. She organized the experiments that were carried out aboard space shuttle *Columbia* on Mission STS-107 in 2003. When *Columbia* exploded during its re-entry into Earth's atmosphere, Chiaki was as shocked and upset as the rest of the world. Although she was sad to lose friends that she had worked with, she decided to continue working in space. Chiaki was looking forward to visiting the International Space Station when it was completed and already had plans for the experiments that she would like to conduct there.

Today, Chiaki lives in the United States and divides her time between working for NASA and working as a Research Instructor in the Department of Surgery at Baylor College of Medicine in Texas. It is only when she returns to Japan that she realizes she has become famous. When she toured her home country after her last mission, crowds followed her wherever she went. "She's surrounded by people who want to touch her and speak with her. She's like a famous film star," said the Japanese ambassador to the United States.

Chapter 10

Kalpana Chawla
1961–2003

On February 1, 2003, in Karnal, India, a group of people gathered in a local school. They were watching a television broadcast of space shuttle *Columbia* as it returned to Earth at the end of Mission STS-107, bringing Kalpana Chawla home. Kalpana was one of the town's heroes, a local girl who had become an astronaut. She hadn't lived in Karnal for years, but she was still a friend, neighbor, and inspiration to those who came together to watch the event.

The mission had been a success, but as the shuttle approached the landing site, something went wrong. The shuttle began to break apart. A few minutes later, it exploded. Kalpana and her crewmates never made it back to Earth.

The people of Karnal were shocked. Instead of celebrating, they mourned Kalpana and tried to comfort one another. Her brother, Sanjay Chawla, was glad that his family was not alone. "This time, such a tragedy has befallen our family, but our relatives and friends and the people of Karnal are all sharing our grief," he said. The people of India felt the loss of Kalpana as much as they had felt pride in her success.

Kalpana was born on July 1, 1961, in Karnal, a city about 75 miles (121 km) northwest of New Delhi, India's capital. She was the youngest of four children. She had two sisters, Sunita and Deepa, but she had little in common with them. She was closest to her brother, Sanjay. They shared an obsession with planes and flying, and they both dreamed of becoming pilots.

Karnal had a flying club, and it was common to see planes and gliders circling over the city. Kalpana and Sanjay would often ride their bicycles after them, looking up at the sky instead of the road and wondering where the planes were going.

Although the family sometimes took rides on the planes, Kalpana was not allowed to take flying lessons. Her father thought that it was too dangerous and that it wasn't appropriate for a girl. Still, Kalpana's obsession with planes grew.

In India, students must commit to a set of subjects, or a "track," when they are about twelve years old. Kalpana decided to focus on engineering, the track that would prepare her for a career in aviation. After high school, she went to Punjab Engineering College to study aeronautical engineering. She was the only woman in her program.

"Aircraft design was really the thing I wanted to pursue," she said. She knew she loved planes and spacecraft, but she was still unsure about where aerospace engineering could lead her. She never thought that it would lead to her becoming an astronaut. "If people asked me what I wanted to do, I remember in the first year I would say, 'I want to be a flight engineer.' But, I am quite sure at that time I didn't have a good idea of what a flight engineer did," she said. Later, she found out that flight engineers navigate planes.

Kalpana's name means "thought" or "imagination."

After her graduation in 1982, Kalpana moved to the United States. She had received job offers in India but she wanted to go to graduate school. "In the back of my mind I knew that the U.S. would have more airplanes than we would at home," she said. Her father didn't want her to go so far from home, but other family members eventually convinced him that moving was the best thing for her.

Because of her father's hesitation, Kalpana almost missed the deadline to register for her classes at the University of Texas, but luckily she made it in time. She earned a master's degree there in 1984 and then went to the University of Colorado-Boulder for her doctorate degree, which she earned in 1988. Kalpana studied aerodynamics, or the way air flows around moving objects.

During this time, she fulfilled her childhood dream of learning to fly planes. Once she started taking lessons, she couldn't stop. Eventually she earned many kinds of licenses, including those for single-engine and multi-engine planes and seaplanes. Maintaining those licenses took a lot of time and money, but to Kalpana it was worth the sacrifices. "I have a very cheap lifestyle in everything else," she

Rakesh Sharma was the first Indian in space. He spent eight days on the Russian space station Mir in 1984.

said, explaining how she managed to afford it. When she became an astronaut years later, she joked, "I hope NASA doesn't find out about the car I drive."

During her first year in the United States, Kalpana met her future husband, a flight instructor named Jean-Pierre Harrison. He was born in Britain, and had immigrated to the United States like Kalpana. They married a year later.

After a few years of doing research in aerodynamics, Kalpana applied to join NASA. The application process can be lengthy, with many stages of interviews and tests, but this doesn't discourage thousands of people from applying every time. Many people apply more than once. Kalpana applied twice to become an astronaut. The first time, she

Like all astronauts, Kalpana trained extensively to learn about the equipment she would be using aboard her shuttle flights. This involved a lot of reading and note-taking!

went as far as taking the medical tests, but in the end she was not accepted. The second time, she made it through all the stages. Waiting to find out if she had been accepted was a nerve-wracking experience. She was excited to have come so close to becoming an astronaut and scared that she might not be accepted for the job. She tried her hardest to figure out when she would be called with the news. In the end, the call came as a surprise.

A NASA official called and calmly asked if she was still interested in working for the space program. Kalpana could not imagine anyone not being interested. "I wanted to tell them then very professionally, 'Oh yes.' But I do remember losing it for just a second," she recalled. Before long, Kalpana and her husband packed up their things, left their jobs, and moved to Houston, Texas, to be close to the Johnson Space Center.

Kalpana enjoyed every minute of the fourteen months she spent training. She was learning new things, challenging herself, and working with people who shared her love of aviation. She became a full astronaut in 1996 and began working on many small, technical projects, each one different from the last. "I could do robotics, work in the computers branch, or be a Cape Crusader," she said. "Cape Crusader" is a nickname for someone who supports shuttle launches from the Kennedy Space Center at Cape Canaveral, Florida.

In November 1996, Kalpana was assigned to her first flight. She would be a mission specialist and primary robotic arm operator on Flight STS-87. A year later, on November 19, 1997, Kalpana became the first Indian woman in space when the shuttle lifted off and began orbiting Earth for sixteen days.

The crew had spent months training for the mission and practicing all their tasks on simulators. Unfortunately, it

wasn't enough to prevent a mistake from happening. One of the crew's tasks was to deploy a satellite, called *Spartan*, which was supposed to collect data from the sun. The plan was to release the satellite from the shuttle and then capture it two days later. It was Kalpana's job to deploy the satellite using the Shuttle Remote Manipulator System.

On the day that *Spartan* was released, everything seemed to be going fine. All of the computer checks were OK as Kalpana sat at the robotic arm controls and got ready to guide *Spartan* out of the payload bay. The satellite was deployed and Kalpana waited for it to rotate. This movement would have shown that the satellite was working properly. *Spartan* didn't move. Kalpana would have to start over. She tried to grab the satellite to put it back in the payload bay. As she touched it with the robotic arm, though, the satellite began spinning, which made it difficult to grab. She kept trying but couldn't get a hold on it. The commander and pilot tried to fly the shuttle so that it would match the satellite's spin. If both the shuttle and *Spartan* were spinning in the same way, the satellite would be easier to catch. This plan didn't work either.

The crew couldn't just abandon the satellite in space. Eventually, two members of the crew performed a space walk and were able to tow *Spartan* into the shuttle manually.

At first, Kalpana was blamed for the mistake because she was the one who was operating the arm when the satellite went out of control. After an investigation, though, NASA found that the mistake was the result of many small errors. "There was no margin of error with the *Spartan* deployment," Kalpana later said. Everything, including the workings of the satellite and the actions of the crew, had to have been perfect, and they weren't.

Kalpana gets fitted for her special orange launch and re-entry suit.

Despite the *Spartan* incident, Kalpana enjoyed her time in space. It felt completely natural to float with nothing touching her or exerting any force on her. "It's not like on Earth where you can feel the ground and your elbows feel that chair. The only thing I fe[lt] is my thoughts," she explained. Partway through the flight, she decided to watch a full rotation of Earth. She sat by the door and watched the planet turn. It only took ninety minutes for the shuttle to circle Earth once. She was impressed by how small Earth is: "An hour and a half and I could go around it. I could do all the math and logic for why this was, but in the big picture the thing that stayed with me is that this place is very small." She became more aware of how important it is to take care of the planet. This is our only home, she realized, and there isn't enough room to make a mess of it.

Columbia was the first space shuttle to be launched into orbit, on April 12, 1981.

Seeing Earth from space was wonderful, but there was more to be being an astronaut than this one experience. The training, the engineering projects, and the flight were equally special to Kalpana. "It is important to me to work hard and have fun doing it," she said. Some people might find some tasks boring or tedious, but Kalpana enjoyed every part of her job.

Her second flight, Mission STS-107, on the space shuttle *Columbia*, blasted off on January 16, 2003. It was a microgravity research flight, and the crew worked non-stop for two weeks doing about eighty different experiments. Many of the experiments were focused on improving cancer

Kalpana keeps up with the enormous amount of science data gathered during Mission STS-107.

medication and treatment. Others looked at how to keep astronauts healthy in space. The experiments went well, and the crew was in high spirits on the day they were to return to Earth. Everyone was excited to be going home.

To begin the journey back, the shuttle's braking rockets fired and *Columbia* fell out of orbit. As a shuttle enters Earth's atmosphere, friction between the shuttle and the atmosphere causes enormous heat. *Columbia*'s entry on February 1 seemed normal at first. Soon, though, sensors were showing that

Kalpana's crewmates on STS-107 were Rick Husband, William McCool, Michael Anderson, David Brown, Laurel Clark, and Ilan Ramon, the first Israeli in space. NASA has created memorials to the crew both on Earth and in space. It named the landing site of one of the Mars rovers Columbia Memorial Station in honor of the crew.

the heat on the left wing was unusually high. Shortly after, mission control stopped receiving temperature data from the left wing. Then radio communication between the shuttle and mission control was lost in the middle of a transmission. Ground control tried for several minutes but could not make contact with the crew. Suddenly, parts of the shuttle broke off and could be seen streaking through the sky. Seconds later, the shuttle exploded, only sixteen minutes before it was supposed to land at the Kennedy Space Center in Florida.

The accident made headlines all over the world. People everywhere mourned the deaths of the seven astronauts who died. NASA immediately set up a commission to learn the cause of the accident. It discovered that during launch, a chunk of foam insulation had broken off one of the external fuel tanks and hit the edge of the shuttle's left wing. Because the shuttle was moving so fast when the foam hit, the foam struck it with a lot of force. The foam damaged the wing's tiles, which are supposed to shield it from the intense heat that the shuttle creates as it shoots down through the atmosphere. When *Columbia* re-entered the atmosphere, the damaged tiles could not protect the wing, which led to the shuttle's explosion.

Kalpana Chawla's death was a tragedy for those who knew her and for those who looked up to her as a role model. Although the journey of her life was cut short, she enjoyed every step of it. She always looked ahead, searching for ways to stretch her boundaries and fulfill her dreams.

Anyone who dreams of becoming an astronaut knows they will face tough odds and competition for acceptance into a space program. Even for the special few who are accepted and finish the years of required training, there are no guarantees that they will make it into space. Nadezhda Vasilievna Kuzhelnaya, a cosmonaut for the Russian Space Agency, was hopeful that she would be one of the lucky ones. Since 1994, she dedicated her life to her dream of reaching space. Unfortunately, the odds were against her.

Nadezhda was born in Alexeevskoe in the Alexeevsky Region of Russia on November 6, 1962. As a child, she loved to watch science-fiction movies and read books about space.

She imagined herself exploring space like the characters in these stories, and she dreamed of becoming a cosmonaut.

When she graduated from high school in 1981, she thought that she wanted to become an architect. She studied at the Dnepropetrovsk Engineering and Building Institute, but when she graduated in 1984 she decided that she was more interested in flying. The flights of the second woman in space, Svetlana Savitskaya, inspired her to pursue a career in space. "I envied her terribly and told myself—why not me?" Nadezhda said. She decided to follow this path and enrolled in the Moscow Aviation Institute. This school trains students to become aircraft, helicopter, and spacecraft engineers. It wasn't exactly the stuff of science-fiction movies, but aviation became her passion.

When she wasn't busy with school, Nadezhda flew planes. She had joined an aviation club in 1981 and tried many types of flying. She began by flying sailplanes, or gliders, which are planes without engines. Eventually, she became such a skilled pilot that she began doing acrobatics. Acrobatics is a difficult and dangerous type of flying. Pilots fly routines that are filled with impressive tricks and maneuvers such as flying upside down, diving, and flying in spirals and loops.

After graduating from the Moscow Aviation Institute in 1988, Nadezhda began working for RKK Energia as an engineer. This company makes the hardware that is used in Russian space flights. Although she was not a cosmonaut yet, designing spacecraft parts allowed her to work with the technology that puts cosmonauts into orbit. She was one step closer to her dream.

"Nadezhda" means "hope" in Russian.

In 1994, she applied to join the cosmonaut team. To her delight, she was selected and she began a two-year process to get ready to go to space. She took a course in general space training at the Yuri Gagarin Cosmonaut Training Center. There, she rode simulators, learned more about spacecraft, and undertook grueling survival exercises.

Partway through her training, Nadezhda got married. Her husband, Vladimir Georgievich Morozov, is a retired military pilot who was Nadezhda's flight instructor. "Nadezhda proved to be a very fast learner and confident student," he says about her.

In 1999, their daughter Ekaterina was born. Nadezhda had to postpone her training for a while, but she returned to work later that year while Vladimir looked after the baby. Nadezhda started preparing to be a flight engineer, the cosmonaut who operates the spacecraft. She would fly a *Soyuz* spacecraft on a "taxi" mission to the International Space Station. Although she had flown many advanced types of aircraft, nothing could compare to flying a *Soyuz*. Versions of these spacecraft have been taking people to space since 1967.

A *Soyuz* spacecraft is always left at the space station in case of an emergency, so that the people living there can escape. This emergency spacecraft does not last very long in the harsh environment of space. It begins to break down as soon as it is delivered. Before the spacecraft becomes unsafe to fly back to Earth, it has to be replaced by a new one. Every six months, a team of three cosmonauts brings a new vehicle

Cosmonaut Elena V. Kondakova, the third Russian woman in space, spent 169 days (more than five months) in space aboard the space station Mir from October 1994 to March 1995. She later flew aboard NASA's *Atlantis* in 1997. On that mission, the shuttle docked with Mir and Elena was able to visit her former home again.

British astronaut Helen Patricia Sharman answered an ad that read "Astronaut wanted—no experience necessary." She flew aboard *Soyuz* TM-12 to the space station Mir in 1991.

to the station and exchanges it for the older one. These taxi missions are one of Russia's contributions to the International Space Station.

Nadezhda was thrilled when she received her first mission in 2001. It seemed as if the years she had spent studying aviation, working on space technology, and training to be a cosmonaut were going to pay off. The closer it got to the mission's launch date, though, the less likely it seemed that she would be making the flight.

Denis Tito, a wealthy American, was willing to pay millions of dollars to be able to go to space. The Russian Space Agency had decided to allow this "space tourist" to make a flight on one of its taxi missions. There was a lot of controversy around the world about whether someone who wasn't a trained astronaut or cosmonaut should be allowed in space. The Russian Space Agency couldn't afford to turn down the money, though. "It was a political decision," Nadezhda says.

Denis Tito did not speak Russian very well, so there had to be an English-speaking cosmonaut on the crew. For Nadezhda, this meant that she was out. On April 28, 2001, the taxi mission took off without her. Later that year, Nadezhda was assigned to be a backup for another flight. She was a backup crew member to French astronaut Claudie Haigneré. Claudie's previous flight in space was in 1996 when she

Modern Russia's space program developed out of the former Soviet Union's space agency. Many of the facilities that are still used today were built during the time of the space race with the United States. In the early 1990s, the Soviet Union broke apart. This change in government created many changes in the country.

A new agency, called Rosaviacosmos (RKA), was formed, but it no longer had the same budget or resources that the Soviet-era agency once enjoyed. Accepting space tourists is one way for RKA to fund its program.

visited the Russian space station Mir. European astronauts like Claudie routinely fly aboard Russian spacecraft. Although this backup assignment did not get Nadezhda to space, she had faith that her next mission would.

The next *Soyuz* missions didn't include her either, though. "The worst thing for me was to watch a spacecraft blasting off without me," she said. Nadezhda began to question why she wasn't being chosen. The process for selecting a crew is complex. Officials must balance the skills and experience of their cosmonauts with their commitments to other space agencies and space

Space tourism continues to grow. Since Denis Tito's flight, South African Mark Shuttleworth has also "vacationed" in space. Lance Bass, of the music group N'SYNC, had also planned on making a flight. Flying on a *Soyuz* to the International Space Station costs about $20 million US. For those with a smaller budget, a training program in Russia is offered for about $10,000.

tourists. When Nadezhda finally got an explanation for why she was being left behind, she strongly objected to one of the reasons she heard. At five feet, four inches tall, officials said she was too short. Because of her height, she does not fit into the type of space suit that cosmonauts wear for space walks.

Nadezhda thought that this reason was nonsense. She had worn the suit during underwater training, when she had put on the suit and diving gear and performed tasks in a tank of water. Although she was "swimming" in the suit as well as the water, Nadezhda was able to do all of the required procedures. "Besides," she says, "none of the 'taxi' missions crew members are expected to do a space walk." There would be no reason for her to wear the space suit. Nadezhda could not hide her disappointment and anger. "Unfortunately," she says, "if a cosmonaut does not fit into

Nadezhda participates in pre-flight training exercises.

a space suit, it is easier for the Russian space authorities to find a replacement for him or her, than for a space suit."

From 1999 to 2004 Nadezhda was the only female cosmonaut. She believes that women are rare because "all space hardware, including space suits and spacecraft comfort assuring systems, were designed mostly by men and for men. For this reason, women do not really fit into the Russian space environment." Throughout her career, Nadezhda has faced challenges because she's a woman. "I would like to be treated like a professional equal to men," she says.

Unfortunately, many people involved with the Russian space program today believe that men should come first in space. Yuri Koptev, head of the Russian Space Agency, has said, "If we decide to send female cosmonauts to the International Space Station, it won't be for a long time.

There will be a place for women cosmonauts aboard the station once the mission teams compromise six or seven people."

Although Nadezhda tried to be patient and waited for years for an opportunity to fly in space, she eventually had to admit that she might be waiting forever. The life of a cosmonaut isn't necessarily a glamorous one, especially for those who haven't flown a mission. Nadezhda received a meager salary that would not increase much until after she made a space flight. She shared cramped living quarters with her husband and daughter in the cosmonaut housing in Star City. In May of 2004, Nadezhda decided that she had waited long enough, and she retired from the cosmonaut corps to take a job as a pilot with Aeroflot, a Russian commercial airline.

"I believe that more women must be admitted to cosmonauts' training in Russia. Women [are] an important driving force behind human civilization's development. If women can be railroad workers in Russia and lay rails on permanent ways, why could they not fly in space?"

–Nadezhda Kuzhelnaya

Despite her disappointment and the financial difficulties she faced while being a cosmonaut, Nadezhda says she would still encourage her daughter to pursue space flight if that were her dream. She and her husband have said, "If Katya wants to fly in space someday, and finds satisfaction in this, she will be blessed by us. It is a true happiness—to do what you want to." Hopefully, by the time Katya is old enough to decide what she wants to do, it won't matter one way or the other that she's a girl.

Glossary

aerodynamics The study of the motion of air and other gaseous fluids and with the forces acting on bodies in motion relative to such fluids.

aeronautics The art and science of designing, making, and operating aircraft.

analyze To examine in detail in order to determine the nature or tendencies of something; to separate a thing or idea into its parts in order to discover their nature, proportion, function, or interrelationship.

astronomy The study of objects and matter outside Earth's atmosphere and of their physical and chemical properties.

astrophysics A branch of astronomy dealing with the behavior, physical properties, and dynamic processes of celestial objects and phenomena.

aviation The art or science of flying airplanes; the development and operation of aircraft.

Capsule Communicator (CAPCOM) Only the Capsule Communicator communicates directly with the crew of a manned space flight. During much of the U.S. manned space program, NASA felt it important for all communication with the astronauts in space to pass through a single individual in the Mission Control Center. That role was designated the Capsule Communicator, or CAPCOM, and was filled by another astronaut, often one of the backup or support crew members. NASA believes that an astronaut is most able to understand the situation in the spacecraft and pass information in the clearest way.

centrifuge A machine using centrifugal force for separating substances of different densities, for removing moisture, or for simulating gravitational effects.

deploy To place something in its appropriate position.

docking The hauling in or guiding into a dock; the joining of two spacecraft.

engineering The science concerned with putting scientific knowledge to practical uses.

extra-vehicular activity (EVA) Work done by an astronaut away from Earth, and outside of a spacecraft, such as a moonwalk or space walk.

flight engineer (FE) A Mission Specialist with additional responsibility of assisting the Pilot and Commander. The FE also keeps track of information from CAPCOM and calls out milestones.

mission specialist A NASA astronaut assigned to a shuttle crew with mission-specific duties.

module An independently operable unit that is a part of the total structure of a space vehicle.

nebula Any of numerous clouds of gas or dust in interstellar space.

optics Any of the elements (such as lenses, mirrors, or light guides) of an optical instrument or system; a science that deals with the genesis (origin) and propagation (spread) of light, the changes that it undergoes and produces, and other phenomena closely associated with it.

payload The load carried by an aircraft or spacecraft consisting of things (such as passengers and instruments) necessary to the purpose of the flight.

payload bay The large central area of the space shuttle orbiter's fuselage in which payloads and their support equipment are carried.

payload specialist Technical experts who accompany specific payloads such as a commercial or scientific satellites.

truss An assemblage of members, such as beams or bands, that form a rigid framework.

For More Information

Astronaut Scholarship Foundation
6225 Vectorspace Boulevard
Titusville, FL 32780
(321) 455-7011
Web site: http://www.astronautscholarship.org

More than eighty astronauts from the Mercury, Gemini, Apollo, Skylab, and other space programs have united to aid the United States in retaining its world leadership in science and technology by providing college scholarships for the very best and brightest students pursuing science, technology, engineering, or math degrees. In addition, the Astronaut Scholarship Foundation (ASF) strongly promotes the importance of science and technology to the general public by facilitating unique programs and special events. Annually, ASF awards twenty-five $10,000 scholarships, and since 1986 has disbursed nearly $3 million to deserving students nationwide.

Canadian Space Agency (CSA)
John H. Chapman Space Centre
6767 Route de l'Aéroport
Saint-Hubert, QC J3Y 8Y9
Canada
(450) 926-4800
Web site: http://www.asc-csa.gc.ca

Established in March 1989, the Canadian Space Agency is committed to leading the development and application of space knowledge for the benefit of Canadians.

European Space Agency (ESA)
8-10 rue Mario Nikis
75738 Paris Cedex 15
France
Tel.: +33 1 5369 7654
Web site: http://www.esa.int/esaCP/index.html
The ESA is Europe's gateway to space. Its mission is to
    shape the development of Europe's space capability and
    ensure that investment in space continues to deliver
    benefits to the citizens of Europe and the world. It is
    an international organization with eighteen Member
    States. By coordinating the financial and intellectual
    resources of its members, it can undertake programs
    and activities far beyond the scope of any single
    European country.

Johnson Space Center
1601 NASA Parkway
Houston, TX 77058
(281) 244-2100
Web site:
    http://www.nasa.gov/centers/johnson/home/index.html
The Johnson Space Center was established in 1961, and
    from the early Gemini, Apollo, and Skylab projects to
    today's space shuttle and International Space Station
    programs and beyond into future space missions, the
    center continues to lead NASA's efforts in human space
    exploration.

Kennedy Space Center
SR 405
Kennedy Space Center, FL 32899
(866) 737-5235

Web site: http://www.kennedyspacecenter.com
NASA's launch headquarters is the only place on Earth
where you can tour launch areas, meet a veteran astronaut, see giant rockets, train in spaceflight simulators,
and even view a launch.

National Aeronautics and Space Administration (NASA)
Public Communications Office
NASA Headquarters, Suite 5K39
Washington, DC 20546-0001
(202) 358-0001
Web site: http://www.nasa.gov
NASA's mission is to reach for new heights and reveal the
unknown to benefit all humankind. NASA has a robust
program of space exploration and operations, flight
technology development, and scientific research.

Russian Federal Space Agency (Roscosmos)
42 Schepkina Street
Moscow, Russia 107996, GSP-6
Tel.: (495) 631-96-12
Web site: http://www.roscosmos.ru
The Federal Space Agency administers Russia's space
assets and manages international cooperation in joint
space projects and programs and the activities of rocket
and space industry entities relating to military space
technologies and strategic missiles. The agency is also
responsible for overall coordination of the activities at
the Baikonur space port.

Smithsonian National Air and Space Museum
National Mall Building
Independence Ave at 6th Street SW
Washington, DC 20560

(202) 633-2214

Web site: http://www.nasm.si.edu

The Smithsonian Institution's National Air and Space Museum maintains the largest collection of historic air and spacecraft in the world. It is also a vital center for research into the history, science, and technology of aviation and space flight, as well as planetary science and terrestrial geology and geophysics.

Web Sites

Due to the changing nature of Internet links, Rosen Publishing has developed an online list of Web sites related to the subject of this book. This site is updated regularly. Please use this link to access the list:

http://www.rosenlinks.com/gwoa/spac

For Further Reading

Bizony, Piers. *The Space Shuttle: Celebrating Thirty Years of NASA's First Space Plane.* Minneapolis, MN: Zenith Press, 2011.

Burgess, Colin. *Selecting the Mercury Seven: The Search for America's First Astronauts.* New York, NY: Springer, 2011.

Dick, Steven, et al., eds. *America in Space: NASA's First Fifty Years.* New York, NY: Abrams, 2007.

Duggins, Pat. *Final Countdown: NASA and the End of the Space Shuttle Program.* Gainesville, FL: University Press of Florida, 2009.

Duggins, Pat. *Trailblazing Mars: NASA's Next Giant Leap.* Gainesville, FL: University Press of Florida, 2010.

Gorn, Michael H. *NASA: The Complete Illustrated History.* London, England: Merrell, 2008.

Grace, N.B. *Women in Space.* North Mankato, MN: Child's World, 2006.

Kevles, Bettyann Holtzmann. *Almost Heaven: The Story of Women in Space.* Cambridge, MA: MIT Press, 2006.

Kranz, Gene. *Failure Is Not an Option: Mission Control from Mercury to Apollo 13 and Beyond.* New York, NY: Simon & Schuster, 2009.

Riddolls, Tom. *Sally Ride: The First American Woman in Space.* New York, NY: Crabtree Publishing, 2010.

Schraff, Anne E. *Ellen Ochoa: Astronaut and Inventor.* Berkeley Heights, NJ: Enslow Publishers, 2009.

Seedhouse, Erik. *Prepare for Launch: The Astronaut Training Process.* New York, NY: Praxis, 2010.

Stone, Tanya Lee. *Almost Astronauts: 13 Women Who Dared to Dream.* Somerville, MA: Candlewick, 2009.

Wearing, Judy. *Roberta Bondar: Canada's First Woman in Space.* New York, NY: Crabtree Publishing Company, 2010.

West, David. *Astronauts* (Graphic Careers). New York, NY: Rosen Publishing, 2008.

Index

A

Armstrong, Neil, 8–9, 58, 75
Atlantis, 61–62, 63–64, 103

B

Bondar, Roberta, 49–57
Bykovsky, Valeri, 35, 36

C

Canadian Space Agency,
    creation of, 52
Cavendish, Margaret, 6
Challenger, 42–46, 47–48, 52
Chawla, Kalpana, 91–100
Cobb, Jerrie, 19–29, 39
Cold War, 30, 31
Coleman, Bessie, 8
Collins, Eileen, 5, 29, 67–73
Columbia, 5, 41, 71–72, 86–88,
    90, 91, 95–97, 98–100
Cunitz, Maria, 6–7

D

Discovery, 54–56, 57, 61, 62–63,
    70–71, 72, 79–81, 89

E

Earhart, Amelia, 8
Endeavor, 82

F

Fleming, Wilhelmina, 7
Funk, Marion Wallace "Wally," 26

G

Gagarin, Yuri, 8, 31, 32, 33,
    34, 35
Glenn, John, 27, 29, 31, 89

H

Hart, Janey, 26
Herschel, Caroline, 11–18
Herschel, William, 13–17, 18
Herschel-Rigollet comet, 16
Hershel, John, 17, 18

I

Imaginary Lines, 48
*Index to Flamsteed's
    Observations of the Fixed
    Stars*, 17
International Space Station,
    62, 63, 64, 76, 77, 78, 79,
    81–82, 90, 103–104, 105,
    106–107

J

Japan Aerospace Exploration
    Agency (JAXA), 85
Jemison, Mae, 60

K

Kondakova, Elena V., 103
Kuzhelnaya, Nadezhda,
    101–107

L

Lovelace, Randy, 22–23, 24, 26

M

McAuliffe, Christa, 47
Mercury Seven, 22, 23, 24–25
Mercury Thirteen, 5, 26, 27, 29
Mir, 52, 70, 71, 76, 93, 103, 105
Mitchell, Marie, 7
Mukai, Chiaki, 83–90

N

NASA, creation of, 22

O

Ochoa, Ellen, 58–66

P

Payette, Julie, 74–82

R

Ride, Sally, 5, 39–48, 58
Rosaviacosmos (RKA), 104
Russian Space Agency, 52,
    101, 104, 106

S

Sally Ride Science, 48
Sharma, Rakesh, 93
Sharman, Helen Patricia, 103
Skylab, 76
Spacelab, 87
space medicine, 51
space motion sickness, 36, 45,
    51, 86
space race, 30, 104
space suits, 42
space tourism, 104, 105
STARSHINE, 81
Sumino, Naoko, 89

T

telescopes, 11, 13, 14, 15, 16
Tereshkova, Valentina, 10, 30–38
Tito, Denis, 104, 105

U

Uranus, discovery of, 15

V

Vostok 5 and *Vostok 6*, 35–36

About the Author

Sonia Gueldenpfennig is a writer, editor, and photographer currently living in Burlington, Ontario. While she isn't an astronaut or even an acrobatic pilot, she gets a similar thrill from whitewater rafting.

Photo Credits

All images in this book are courtesy of NASA with the exception of the following: